Sustainable Development and International Food Trade Policies

With a particular focus on developing economies, this book explores the intersection between agri-environmental policy, food policy, agricultural trade policy, and sustainable development. This book explores the many factors which shape sustainable development policies in agriculture. On the production side, using environmentally friendly inputs and good agricultural practices to protect the land and other related resources are necessary conditions for sustainable agriculture. On the other hand, ensuring food safety, security, and sustainable consumption are necessary elements of sustainable food policies and development. In addition, as the agricultural sector grows in an economy, energy needs become a major issue, especially for countries that depend on import. This book explores how these elements are balanced – along with global factors such as foreign direct investment, international climate change provisions, and the role of the WTO – in domains such as value chains, biotechnology, gender equality, ecology, and trade-environment interaction. This book will be of great interest to advanced readers in the fields of agricultural policy, food trade policy, and sustainable development.

Cemal Atici is a professor of agricultural economics at Aydin Adnan Menderes University, Türkiye.

Routledge Studies in Agricultural Economics

Series Editor: Ashok Mishra, *Arizona State University, USA*

Public Policy in Agriculture
Impact on Labor Supply and Household Income
Edited by Ashok K. Mishra, Davide Viaggi and Sergio Gomez y Paloma

Agricultural Development in Brazil
The Rise of a Global Agro-food Power
Edited by Antonio M. Buainain, Rodrigo Lanna and Zander Navarro

The Economics of Food Loss in the Produce Industry
Edited by Travis Minor, Suzanne Thornsbury, and Ashok K. Mishra

Transforming Agriculture in South Asia
The Role of Value Chains and Contract Farming
Edited by Ashok K. Mishra, Anjani Kumar and Pramod K. Joshi

Sustainability in Agribusiness
The Impact of Societal Challenges, Technological Advancements, and
Development Goals
Edited by Maria Carmela Annosi, Francesco Appio, and Federica Brunetta

Sustainable Development and International Food Trade Policies
Cemal Atici

For more information about this series, please visit: www.routledge.com/
Routledge-Studies-in-Agricultural-Economics/book-series/RSAG

Sustainable Development and International Food Trade Policies

Cemal Atici

Routledge
Taylor & Francis Group

LONDON AND NEW YORK

First published 2024
by Routledge
4 Park Square, Milton Park, Abingdon, Oxon OX14 4RN

and by Routledge
605 Third Avenue, New York, NY 10158

Routledge is an imprint of the Taylor & Francis Group, an informa business

© 2024 Cemal Atici

British Library Cataloguing-in-Publication Data
A catalogue record for this book is available from the British Library

Library of Congress Cataloging-in-Publication Data
Names: Atici, Cemal, author.
Title: Sustainable development and international food trade policies /
Cemal Atici.
Description: Abingdon, Oxon ; New York, NY : Routledge, 2024. |
Series: Routledge studies in agricultural economics | Includes bibliographical
references and index. |
Identifiers: LCCN 2023055589 (print) | LCCN 2023055590 (ebook) |
ISBN 9781032708515 (hardback) | ISBN 9781032708546 (paperback) |
ISBN 9781032708577 (ebook)
Subjects: LCSH: Sustainable development—Developing countries. | Nutrition
policy—Developing countries.
Classification: LCC HC59.72.E5 A85 2024 (print) | LCC HC59.72.E5
(ebook) | DDC 338.9/27091724—dc23/eng/20231221
LC record available at https://lccn.loc.gov/2023055589
LC ebook record available at https://lccn.loc.gov/2023055590

ISBN: 9781032708515 (hbk)
ISBN: 9781032708546 (pbk)
ISBN: 9781032708577 (ebk)

DOI: 10.4324/9781032708577

Typeset in Times New Roman
by Codemantra

Contents

Tables and Figures

Tables

Figures

About the Author

Atici is a professor of agricultural economics at Aydin Adnan Menderes University. He received his Ph.D. in agricultural economics from Louisiana State University. He conducted studies on food trade, development, and environmental economics at various international organizations. His current studies include food safety policies, trade, and sustainable development.

Preface

Sustainable development requires designing and implementing specific policies. Sustainable food trade policies are especially important in today's world in achieving specific goals such as food security, food safety, and adequate income levels for the producers while protecting and improving the environmental quality. Although there are many dynamics of sustainable food trade policies, there is a need for a complete study that combines all the perspectives of these policies to better understand the issues and factors interacting with each other. Therefore, this book aims to contribute to the field of food trade policy by examining the linkages and interactions of sustainable food trade policies. This book can serve as a resource for graduate studies, policymakers, and professionals in the fields of agricultural policy, food trade policy, and sustainable development.

1 Introduction

Sustainable development requires designing and implementing specific policies in each related sector. Constructing a framework and determining the interactions are necessary for better understanding the issue and implementing sustainable policies. Sustainable development is traditionally defined as "development that meets the needs of the present without compromising the ability of future generations to meet their own needs."[1] Much of the argument is focused on the concept of development, such as the tradeoff between current and future welfare, which is the subject of the growth models.[2] In terms of agricultural development, equity, resilience, and efficiency are three main concepts, and valuation, regulation, and monitoring are essential to achieve sustainable agricultural development.[3] Full-cost, cost-effectiveness, property rights, and sustainability principles can alleviate the environmental problems faced.[4] The concept of sustainable development has been criticized for being too vague and too late to address the issues faced.[5] However, the sustainable development decision-making framework is still a comprehensive approach to today's problems.[6]

Certain theoretical concepts shape sustainable development on a global scale.[7] These concepts can be classified as global civil society, regime theory, and global environmental governance. The global civil society consists of nongovernmental organizations (NGOs). The meaning of civil society has evolved over the years and has been shaped by global events.[8] The regime theory argues that international institutions and regimes shape the behaviors of the states in the decision-making process, allowing cooperation. The idea aims to explain the factors why states undertake collective action in the international system instead of a solidary approach.[9] Global environmental governance is the sum of organizations, related policy instruments, financing mechanisms, procedures, and norms that aim to regulate the processes of international environmental protection.[10] The NGOs seek to influence both formal treaty organizations and related documents such as declarations, reports, and commitments.[11]

The interaction between the concepts mentioned and sustainable development provides specific outcomes to better understand the linkage. The use

DOI: 10.4324/9781032708577-1

of appropriate technology is essential for sustainable development; however, traditional technologies and institutions are insufficient to achieve the goals. Promoting coordination between NGOs and research institutions is vital to achieve sustainable development goals.[12] In addition, community-generated information can be utilized in developing countries' project planning and climate adaptation strategies.[13]

Global considerations and international initiatives significantly impact a country's policy designs. As economies become increasingly integrated, new institutions of global governance shape political and economic behavior. Therefore, sustainable agricultural development is also significantly determined by the emerging international rules governing trade and the environment.[14] In designing sustainable policies, especially in developing regions related to institutional designs such as public investments in infrastructure, human capital and technology for competitiveness, phasing of policy reforms for adjustment periods, and safety nets are essential.[15]

There are many drivers of sustainable development. Food trade policies in that context are interrelated with various major factors and sub-factors that affect sustainable development. Examining the linkages can provide helpful insights into formulating and designing sustainable policies in food and agriculture. Sustainable food trade policies interact with many other drivers, such as conventional trade policies, non-tariff measures (NTMs), food safety, food security, aid for trade, trade facilitation, sustainability standards, gender, foreign direct investment (FDI), and climate change. Therefore, after presenting the related framework, this book examines the linkages, citing the related and most recent studies, and discusses the possible solutions to the issues faced in the sustainable food trade policy setting.

Notes

1 WCED, Report of the World Commission on Environment and Development: Our Common Future, (1987).
2 Anil Markandya, "Criteria for Sustainable Agricultural Development," in Anil Markandya and Julie Richardson, eds, *Environmental Economics: A Reader*, (New York: St. Martin's Press, 1993).
3 For a detailed discussion of the issue see Markandya (1993).
4 Tom Tietenberg, *Environmental and Natural Resource Economics* (New York: HarperCollins Publishers, 1992).
5 See Dernbach and Cheever (2015) for a detailed discussion on the critiques.
6 John Dernbach, Federico Cheever, "Sustainable development and its discontents," *Transnational Environmental Law*, 4(2), (2015):247–287.
7 For a detailed discussion on the sustainable development theory see Egelston (2013).
8 Mary Kaldor, "The idea of global civil society," *International Affairs*, 79(3), (2003):583–593.
9 Anne E. Egelston, *Sustainable Development. A History* (Dordrecht: Springer, 2013).
10 Adil Najam, et al., *Global Environmental Governance A Reform Agenda* (Winnipeg: IISD, 2006).

11 Egelston, *Sustainable Development*, 48–54.
12 David Kaimowitz, "The role of nongovernmental organizations in agricultural research and technology transfer in Latin America," *World Development*, 21(7), (1993):1139–1150.
13 Patrick Pringle, Declan Conway, "Voices from the frontline: The role of community-generated information in delivering climate adaptation and development objectives at project level," *Climate and Development*, 4(2), (2012):104–113.
14 Luc Juillet, et al. "Sustainable agriculture and global institutions: Emerging institutions and mixed incentives," *Society & Natural Resources*, 10(3), (1997):309–318.
15 Arie Kuyvenhoven, "Creating an enabling environment: Policy conditions for less-favored areas," *Food Policy*, 29(4), (2004):407–429.

References

Dernbach, J., Cheever, F. (2015). Sustainable development and its discontents. *Transnational Environmental Law*, 4(2), 247–287.

Egelston, A. (2013). *Sustainable Development. A History.* Dordrecht: Springer.

Juillet, L., Roy, J., Scala, F. (1997). Sustainable agriculture and global institutions: Emerging institutions and mixed incentives. *Society & Natural Resources*, 10(3), 309–318.

Kaimowitz, D. (1993). The role of nongovernmental organizations in agricultural research and technology transfer in Latin America. *World Development*, 21(7), 1139–1150.

Kaldor, M. (2003). The idea of global civil society. *International Affairs*, 79(3), 583–593.

Kuyvenhoven, A. (2004). Creating an enabling environment: Policy conditions for less-favored areas. *Food Policy*, 29(4), 407–429.

Markandya, A. (1993). Criteria for Sustainable Agricultural Development, in A. Markandya, J. Richardson, eds. *Environmental Economics: A Reader*. New York: St. Martin's Press.

Najam, A., Papa, M., Taiyap, N. (2006). *Global Environmental Governance: A Reform Agenda*. Winnipeg: IISD.

Pringle, P., Conway, D. (2012). Voices from the frontline: The role of community-generated information in delivering climate adaptation and development objectives at project level. *Climate and Development*, 4(2), 104–113.

Tietenberg, T. (1992). *Environmental and Natural Resource Economics*. New York: HarperCollins Publishers.

WCED (1987). Report of the World Commission on Environment and Development: Our Common Future. https://sustainabledevelopment.un.org/content/documents/5987our-common-future.pdf [Accessed October 20, 2022].

Part I

Development Theories and Sustainable Development

2   Development Theories and Agriculture

Although almost every nation wants to prosper as an ideal, the methods to achieve the goal of development differ because of different ideologies. The root of development theories goes back to the theoretical development of political economy and extends to current critics of conventional modernization.[1] It is essential to understand the basic foundations of some of the important theories related to the development. Therefore, this section mainly addresses the relevant growth and development theories and their interaction with sustainable agricultural development.

The primary argument of the cyclical economic development developed by Schumpeter claims that an economy is constantly transformed by disruption and innovation. Therefore, this view of economic development presents a dynamic system compared to the static equilibrium approaches of the previous classical theories. The spontaneous changes in an economy are caused by productive innovations such as new goods, methods, markets, and organizations.[2] In today's world, achieving climate and environmental goals in the context of sustainable development may require regulation-induced innovation, deployment, and diffusion rather than an evolutionary economic process. Stringent regulations can stimulate the application of environmentally beneficial products and technologies. The diffusion of sustainable technologies, on the other hand, is essential in promoting sustainable practices in many sectors, including the sector of agriculture.[3] In one of the studies testing the creative destruction theory for a forest bioeconomy,[4] it was found that an effective policy mix combines climate mitigation policies with sustainable forest management policies, research and development policies, and awareness-raising policies. Technology-based ventures and entrepreneurship are essential factors in sustainable development. Total entrepreneurship activities related to technology sectors may improve sustainability in the long run.[5]

As an early Keynesian growth model, the Harrod-Domar model attempted to examine the cause of growth based on savings and capital levels, implying that more investment leads to capital accumulation and growth. The model

DOI: 10.4324/9781032708577-2

was extended by Solow, stating that long-term growth is possible with technological progress.[6] Various studies examining the interaction between related growth models and sustainable development provided useful insights into policy design. For instance, a study examining the augmented green Solow model found that risk and uncertainty factors have significant short and long-run effects on sustainable development and underlined the importance of risk management in sustainable policy design.[7] Given the fact that certain developing countries' development progress has a negative impact on environmental quality, the tradeoff between economic development and emission levels sets a challenge in climate agreements.[8]

The differences in the structure of traded commodities can affect the terms of trade and overall welfare. The Prebisch-Singer thesis[9] argues that in the long run, prices of primary commodities decline relative to the prices of manufactured commodities, leading to the deterioration of terms of trade in some developing countries that export mainly primary commodities. Therefore, this theory implies diversification in economic activity and export structure for improvements in welfare. The implication of this thesis is arguable and tested by various studies. For instance, some studies examining the long-term trend of primary commodities found no evidence,[10] while others found specific evidence for it.[11] In addition, commodity price movements have an asymmetric country effect on economic activity such that low commodity prices benefit developed countries but depress growth in some developing countries.[12] Given that sustainable development requires diversification in economic activities, especially agriculture, a modern interpretation of this thesis can provide a certain level of insight into sustainable policy designs.

Recent endogenous growth models[13] assume that long-term economic growth is determined by internal factors such as investment in human capital and innovation. Therefore, these models favor research and development support and various incentives for innovations. A study examining the endogenous growth-sustainable development interaction found that the short-run effects of environmental policies differ substantially from the long-run effects. There is a tradeoff between growth and environmental quality in the long run.[14] In another study examining the impact of a technological change on sustainable development, it is stated that technological change has the potential to compensate for natural resource scarcity and diminishing returns to capital but is limited to certain restrictions such as rising research costs.[15] A recent study examining the impact of economic growth and international trade on resource conservation and depletion[16] found that international trade impacts resource conservation or depletion of natural resources, and widening international trade can lead countries to shift from conservation to depletion.

Indeed, new growth theories can help better understand the interaction between technological progress and sustainable development. Investment in human capital, research and development, and productive public investment toward cleaner technologies can be used in sustainable policy designs to improve environmental quality. Certainly, some of these policies are difficult to design and implement, especially for low-income developing countries. However, setting priorities in strategic planning and capacity development through international cooperation yields long-term benefits and improves welfare. In that context, institutional structuring of rural stakeholders and efficient interaction among them is necessary for a stable development process. Above all, the related legal infrastructure needs to be established, covering related issues and parties in line with global developments. Such a structural change can be achieved through international aid for capacity development and regional initiatives such as South-South Cooperation (SSC). In addition, regional economic integrations can facilitate information exchange and collaboration among the members. In agriculture, such cooperation is especially feasible in the areas of climate change mitigation, developing projects for renewable energy, and coping with food safety measures in agricultural trade. Partnership in international agricultural trade through trade agreements and technical aid, in that sense, is especially important given the fact that agriculture plays a crucial role in developing countries' economic development.

3 Sustainable Development and Food Trade

An overview of world agricultural trade by region is presented in Figure 3.1. According to the data,[17] the shares of Eastern Africa, Central Asia, Northern America, Western Europe, and Oceania in total world agricultural exports have declined over the period. South America, Southern Asia, Western Asia, and Eastern Europe all have increased their shares over the period mentioned. The export unit value index (EUVI) and import value index (IUVI), with a base period of 2014–2016, increased in all regions at different levels (Figures 3.2 and 3.3). For instance, IUVI increased noticeably in most of the regions in Africa, South America, Southern Asia, and Eastern Europe compared to the year 2000. On the other hand, based on the export and import unit values (EUVI, IUVI), the terms of trade values have implied an improvement in the regions of Western Africa, Eastern Asia, Northern America, Europe, and Oceania, while a deterioration in some regions such as most of the regions in Africa, Central-Southern Asia, and Eastern Europe due to relatively higher level of increases in IUVI. The relatively higher share of processed food imports in total agricultural imports is one of the factors in high import unit prices in some regions.[18]

Since a rise in terms of trade increases a country's welfare, the gains can be utilized in improving capacity development and achieving sustainable development goals. Food trade policies can be designed efficiently so that they can contribute to sustainable development goals. Efficient trade policies include optimal import and export policies in line with the multilateral trading

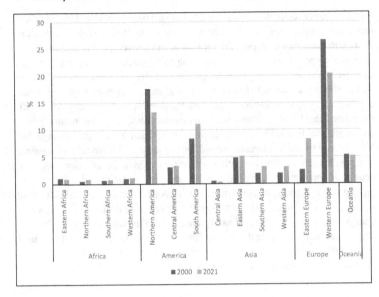

Figure 3.1 The Shares of Agricultural Exports in World Total Agricultural Exports by Selected Region, 2000–2021

Source: FAOSTAT, 2023.

system so that higher social welfare is obtained. Utilization of the appropriate non-tariff measures, such as food safety regulations, and controlling and monitoring of biotechnology in agricultural systems ensure cleaner production systems and healthy consumption for society. Certain food trade policies, such as trade facilitation, will assure food security when implemented on time. Global value chains, by coordinating the private-public partnership, monitoring, and stakeholder participation, benefit sustainable agricultural production and improve trade potential. The use of appropriate technology improves production and trade capacity, assuring food security. For instance, a study examining technological innovation in sub-Saharan Africa[19] found that agricultural technological improvement in the region would increase world trade volume, wages, and welfare, reducing food insecurity.

Well-designed environmental regulations covering food trade policies both protect domestic consumers and encourage producers in exporting countries to produce in accordance with the rules and regulations that improve the environmental quality. However, although environmental regulations in imported food products reduce environmental pressure, growth in consumption may offset the gains, especially in some developed countries.[20] Therefore,

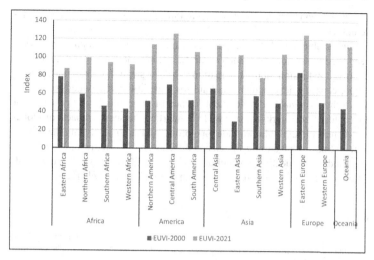

Figure 3.2 Agricultural Export Unit Value Index by Region, 2000–2021
Source: FAOSTAT, 2023.

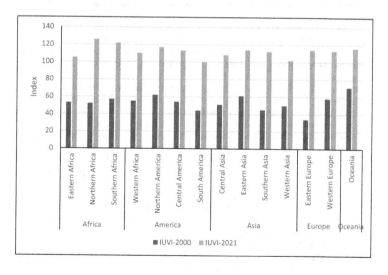

Figure 3.3 Agricultural Import Unit Value Index by Region, 2000–2021
Source: FAOSTAT, 2023.

sustainable consumption is also essential in achieving global sustainable development goals.

Sustainable development policies, especially in developing countries, need to address wider areas such as rural development, land reform, financing, improved extension, and participation.[21] In that stage, international collaboration, capacity development, and aid for trade initiatives evidently contribute to the sustainable development agenda of developing countries. Recent conceptual frameworks in food trade[22] underline the social impacts of global value chains in agricultural trade on a product basis. In analyzing the impact of food trade, related multi-dimensional factors, such as nutrition, health, living standards, education, and cultural values, therefore need to be addressed. Some of these issues will be examined in detail in the next chapters.

Notes

1 For a detailed review of the theories of development see Peet and Hartwick (1999).

2 Richard Peet, Elaine Hartwick, *Theories of Development* (New York: The Guilford Press, 1999).

3 Nicholas A. Ashford, Ralph P. Hall, "Achieving global climate and environmental goals by governmental regulatory targeting," *Ecological Economics*, 152, (2018):246–259.

4 Luana Ladu, et al., "The role of the policy mix in the transition toward a circular forest bioeconomy," *Forest Policy and Economics*, 110, (2020):1–17.

5 Islem Khefacha, Lotfi Belkacem, "Technology-based ventures and sustainable development: Cointegrating and causal relationships with a panel data approach," *Journal of International Trade and Economic Development*, 25(2), (2016):192–212.

6 Richard Peet, Elaine Hartwick, *Theories of Development*, 39–40.

7 Ahmed I. Hunjra, et al., "Sustainable development: The impact of political risk, macroeconomic policy uncertainty and ethnic conflict," *International Review of Financial Analysis*, 84, (2022):1–11.

8 Shyam Ranganathan, Ranjula B. Swain, "Sustainable development and global emission targets: A dynamical systems approach to aid evidence-based policy making," *Sustainable Development*, 26(6), (2019):812–821.

9 Raul Prebisch, The *Economic Development of Latin America and Its Principal Problems* (New York: United Nations, 1950); Hans W. Singer, "The US foreign investment in underdeveloped areas: The distribution of gains between investing and borrowing countries," *American Economic Review*, 40, (1950):473–485.

10 John T. Cuddington, "Long-run trends in 26 primary commodity prices: A disaggregated look at the Prebisch-Singer hypothesis," *Journal of Development Economics*, 39(2), (1992):207–227; Atanu Ghoshray, "A reexamination of trends in primary commodity prices," *Journal of Development Economics*, 95(2), (2011):242–251.

11 See Sapsford and Balasubramanyam (1992); Bloch and Sapsford (1997); Bloch and Sapsford (2000); Kellard and Wohar (2006); Erten and Ocampo (2013) for the detailed information on the estimation issues.

12 David I. Harvey, et al., "Long-run commodity prices, economic growth, and interest rates: 17th century to the present day," *World Development*, 89, (2017):57–70.

13 See Romer (1986); Lucas (1988) on the endogenous growth models.

14 A. Lans Bovenberg, Sjak A. Smulders, "Transitional impacts of environmental policy in an endogenous growth models," *International Economic Review*, 37(4), (1996):861–893.

15 Lucas Bretschger, "Economics of technological change and the natural environment: How effective are innovations as a remedy for resource scarcity? *Ecological Economics*, 54(2–3), (2004):148–163.

16 Marie-Catherine Riekhof, et al., "Economic growth, international trade, and the depletion or conservation of renewable natural resources," *Journal of Environmental Economics and Management*, 97, (2019):116–133.

17 See FAOSTAT (2023).

18 Comtrade (2023).

19 Mihasina H. Andrianarimanana, Pu Yongjian, "Importance of the improvement in the agricultural technology of sub-Saharan Africa on local economic development and international trade," *Sustainability*, 13(2555), (2001):1–14.

20 Philipp Schepelmann, et al., "Driving forces of changing environmental pressures from consumption in the European food system," *Sustainability*, 12(9), (2020):8265 (1–30).

21 Fantu Cheru, "Structural adjustment, primary resource trade and sustainable development in sub-Saharan Africa," *World Development*, 20(4), (1992):497–512.

22 Marije Schaafsma, et al., "A framework to understand the social impacts of agricultural trade," *Sustainable Development*, 31(1), (2023):138–150.

References

Andrianarimanana, M.H., Yongjian, P. (2021). Importance of the improvement in the agricultural technology of sub-Saharan Africa on local economic development and international trade. *Sustainability*, 13(2555), 1–14.

Ashford, N.A., Hall, R.P. (2018). Achieving global climate and environmental goals by governmental regulatory targeting. *Ecological Economics*, 152, 246–259.

Bloch, H., Sapsford, D. (1997). Some estimates of Prebisch and Singer effects on the terms of trade between primary producers and manufacturers. *World Development*, 25(11), 1873–1884.

Bloch, H., Sapsford, D. (2000). Whither the terms of trade? An elaboration of the Prebisch-Singer hypothesis. *Cambridge Journal of Economics*, 24(4), 461–181.

Bovenberg, A.L., Smulders, S.A. (1996). Transitional impacts of environmental policy in an endogenous growth models. *International Economic Review*, 37(4), 861–893.

Bretschger, L. (2004). Economics of technological change and the natural environment: How effective are innovations as a remedy for resource scarcity? *Ecological Economics*, 54(2–3), 148–163.

Cheru, F. (1992). Structural adjustment, primary resource trade and sustainable development in sub-Saharan Africa. *World Development*, 20(4), 497–512.

Comtrade (2023). UN Comtrade Database. https://comtradeplus.un.org/TradeFlow [Accessed September 21, 2023].

Cuddington, J.T. (1992). Long-run trends in 26 primary commodity prices: A disaggregated look at the Prebisch-Singer hypothesis. *Journal of Development Economics*, 39(2), 207–227.

Erten, B., Ocampo, J.A. (2013). Super cycles of commodity prices since the mid-nineteenth century. *World Development*, 44, 14–30.

FAOSTAT (2023). http://www.fao.org/faostat [Accessed September 27, 2023].

Ghoshray, A. (2011). A reexamination of trends in primary commodity prices. *Journal of Development Economics*, 95(2), 242–251.

Harvey, D.I., Kellard, N.M., Madsen, J.B., Wohar, M.E. (2017). Long-run commodity prices, economic growth, and interest rates: 17th century to the present day. *World Development*, 89, 57–70.

Hunjra, A., Azam, M., Burna, M.G., Verhoeven, P., Al-Faryan, M.A.S. (2022). Sustainable development: The impact of political risk, macroeconomic policy uncertainty and ethnic conflict. *International Review of Financial Analysis*, 84, 1–11.

Kellard, N., Wohar, M.E. (2006). On the prevalence of trends in primary commodity prices. *Journal of Development Economics*, 79(1), 146–167.

Khefacha, I., Belkacem, L. (2016). Technology-based ventures and sustainable development: Cointegrating and causal relationships with a panel data approach. *Journal of International Trade and Economic Development*, 25(2), 192–212.

Ladu, L., Imbert, E., Quitzow, R., Morone, P. (2020). The role of the policy mix in the transition toward a circular forest bioeconomy. *Forest Policy and Economics*, 110, 1–17.

Lucas, R.E. (1988). On the mechanics of economic development. *Journal of Monetary Economics*, 22, 3–42.

Peet, R., Hartwick, E. (1999). *Theories of Development*. New York: The Guilford Press.

Prebisch, R. (1950). *The Economic Development of Latin America and its Principal Problems*. New York: United Nations.

Ranganathan, S., Swain, R.B. (2019). Sustainable development and global emission targets: A dynamical systems approach to aid evidence-based policy making. *Sustainable Development*, 26(6), 812–821.

Riekhof, M.C., Regnier, E., Quass, M.F. (2019). Economic growth, international trade, and the depletion or conservation of renewable natural resources. *Journal of Environmental Economics and Management*, 97, 116–133.

Romer, P.M. (1986). Increasing returns and long-run growth. *Journal of Political Economy*, 94(5), 1002–1037.

Sapsford, D., Balasubramanyam, V.N. (1994). The long-run behavior of the relative price of primary commodities: Statistical evidence and policy implications. *World Development*, 22(11), 1737–1745.

Schaafsma, M., Dreoni, I., Ayompe, L.M., Egoh, B., Ekayana, D.P., Favareto, A., Mumbunan, S., Nakagawa, L., Ngouhouo-poufoun, J., Sassen, M., Uehara, T.K., Matthews, Z. (2023). A framework to understand the social impacts of agricultural trade. *Sustainable Development*, 31(1), 138–150.

Schepelmann, P., Vercalsteren, A., Acosta-Fernandez, J., Saurat, M., Boonen, K., Christis, M., Marin, G., Zoboli, R., Maguire, C. (2020). Driving forces of changing environmental pressures from consumption in the European food system. *Sustainability*, 12(19), 8265 (1–30).

Singer, H.W. (1950). The US foreign investment in underdeveloped areas: The distribution of gains between investing and borrowing countries. *American Economic Review*, 40, 473–485.

Part II

Political Economy of Sustainable Food Policies and Trade

4 Political Economy of Food Policies and Trade

Agriculture is supported differently in various countries. There are many factors that affect the decision of support, such as the share of agriculture in national income, the distribution of the labor force, the weight of interest groups, and lobbying. The political economy models, such as interest group approaches, median-voting model, and game theory, examine the factors that shape political decisions in developed and developing countries.

Lobbying through interest groups can impact the design and outcomes of policies in agriculture. In some cases, the lobbying efforts of interest groups are reflected more closely in external policy design, while in some cases, external food policy is much more independent of interest group pressures and rather is shaped by common regional policies.[1] A study examining global food policies found that democratization leads to a reduction of agricultural taxation and an increase in agricultural subsidization underlying the predictions of the median voter model because political transitions occurred primarily in countries with a majority of farmers.[2] The main factors that influence the systematic subsidization of wheat producers in developed countries are the labor productivity ratio, agriculture's international terms of trade, and the share of food in disposable income. On the other hand, the factor endowment ratio, agriculture's international terms of trade, and the share of imports financed by agricultural exports are the most important factors contributing to the systematic exploitation of wheat producers in developing countries.[3] The role of the sharing economy (SE) also has some major implications for sustainable agriculture. For instance, the proposed SE-based mechanism can deliver greater financial gains with higher sustainable development benefits when designed and implemented appropriately due to its peer-to-peer sharing features.[4]

Public policies usually have four main goals: equity, efficiency, security, and liberty.[5] Achieving these goals in today's globalized world is complex and requires carefully designed policies. These goals certainly interact with each other, and there are some tradeoffs among them.[6] In that sense, the interaction of the policy goals and sustainable development in the context of food trade

DOI: 10.4324/9781032708577-3

is quite important. Although most of the trade theories examined the welfare gains of trade liberalization,[7] the income distribution aspect has received less attention. The main argument of the classical theories underlines the efficient use of resources and, consequently, welfare gains caused by free trade.

On the other hand, the imperfect structure of international markets questions the implication of trade policies as mentioned above. The quantitative studies examining the issue utilizing various methods can shed light on the discussion. In a country that exports primary goods and imports manufactured goods, an open strategy might worsen income distribution since lower manufacturing prices caused by lower exchange rates lead to higher imports in sectors that benefit wealthy groups more. However, for a country that exports manufactured goods and imports food, a liberal policy helps income distribution because an open development strategy such as an increase in exports would lead to a lower effective exchange rate, which in turn would lower the relative price of food imports that has a greater influence on the expenditures of the low-income socioeconomic groups.[8] From the historical perspective, a study found that globalization increases inequality between nations but that globalization has no significant effect within nations. In the countries that liberalized their policies, welfare gains were observed, but those who were isolated did not gain substantial welfare gains.[9]

Economic integrations also affect the distribution of income in an economy. Economic integrations may improve welfare, but the income distribution within the agricultural sector becomes less equal with the integration. In addition, a Pareto optimal solution does not imply an equitable solution for the parties involved. In that context, income distributional effects should be evaluated in policy analysis, given that trade policies affect the welfare distribution within an economy as they affect the welfare of various interest groups.[10] A decrease in agricultural protection and liberalization in developing countries might generate significant welfare gains but hurt the rural population; therefore, government compensation is necessary.[11] Certainly, trade liberalization alone may not be sufficient to reduce poverty and inequality, and specific domestic policies aiming for equality are needed, especially in developing countries. Given the fact that government resources are limited in many developing countries, sector-specific compensations such as direct income support can be used.[12] In the implementation of these kinds of policies, it should be kept in mind that the programs should only last for a stipulated period[13] in order to prevent excessive budgetary burdens and provide a smooth transition. Trade liberalization is expected to improve efficiency in a country. Trade can benefit importers to access better inputs utilized in production, and exporters can improve themselves through competition. In addition, as policies are liberalized, factors of production move to more efficient sectors and increase production in those sectors. A study examining the trade-efficiency interaction[14] suggests that the efficiency difference between foreign and domestic inputs has a major effect on productivity gains, and the declines in tariff rates significantly raise productivity growth.

From the sustainable development perspective, the choice of optimal level of output differs in terms of the definition of optimality, and it is essential to consider the opportunity costs of resources.[15] An increase in production through liberalization may lead to the exploitation of resources, causing ecological problems. Biodiversity can be affected negatively by increasing trade activities.[16] The most recent study[17] revealed that the current global land use leads to the loss of endemic species worldwide. Trade affects biodiversity losses through developmental pressure, market failure, and intervention failure.[18] As free trade expands, increasing pressure causes natural resources to be overly exploited. Developing countries are especially much more vulnerable to this kind of pressure due to their flora and fauna endowments. Trade can stimulate the transfer of these resources for medical, health, and pharmaceutical reasons. Therefore, regulations, controls, and monitoring are required. Improper property rights assignments and externalities may lead to market failure. Well-defined property rights and property rights assignments are crucial in developing countries and are closely related to other structural adjustments in a society, such as legal and political regulations. Externalities exist when the well-being of an agent depends on the activities of other agents. These externalities cause inefficiencies because while they might increase the surplus of one agent, they might also cause damage to society, causing environmental problems. Hence, trade liberalization and environment interaction should be evaluated carefully in public policy design.[19]

5   Trade Policies and Sustainability

Trade policies can be used as powerful instruments for sustainable development goals. Traditional trade theories are based on differences in technology and factor endowments and thus recommend the specialization in low-cost sectors and encourage free trade. However, new trade theories[20] based on the economics of scale and imperfect competition exhibited a different approach, implying that protective measures can be used to favor new industries. These theories gave rise to the strategic trade policy and intra-industry trade concept in the development agenda.[21]

Trade benefits sustainable development in agriculture, providing food security. However, domestic policies distorting trade, such as subsidies, may negatively impact the smallholders in developing countries and harm diversification in production. A detailed discussion is presented in the food security section. If trade policy instruments are used mainly for trade-related strategies, their impacts will be more efficient. The use of trade policies for secondary purposes (i.e., employment, domestic production goals), on the other hand, will lead to efficiency loss in terms of the use of natural resources. It is essential that the use of conventional trade protection policies and the NTMs are in line with the development agenda of the multilateral trading system, addressing the needs of developing countries, and these policies should not construct barriers to trade.

New growth theories that treat technology as endogenous emphasize investment in human capital, knowledge, innovation, R&D, and spillover effects in economic development.[22] The spillovers from public agricultural R&D can improve the agricultural sector by mitigating market failures.[23] These theories have a certain level of implications for trade and sustainable development. Technology can be transferred internationally through trade[24] and help developing countries with their long-term growth. In addition, the adverse welfare impacts of unilateral trade liberalization may be compensated by the productivity advantages of embodied technological spillovers.[25] However, it should be noted that this is not an easy task, and although some technology transfers through FDI bring cleaner technologies replacing the polluting ones, it is possible that it may bring the old and polluting technologies which lead to pollution havens. For instance, the difference in environmental regulations may provide a comparative advantage in pollution-intensive production among countries.[26] Thus, sustainable policies require well-designed regulations, environmentally friendly and efficient technologies, regional partnerships, and research and development expenditures in that area to improve environmental quality.

5.1   *Imperfect Competition, Trade Policy, and Agriculture*

Although we have mentioned imperfect competition, it is better to expand the imperfect market structure and trade policy issues a little more based on the fact that international markets, including food trade, display imperfect structures.[27] Beginning from a conventional tariff analysis, in perfectly competitive markets, imposing tariffs in a small economy raises domestic prices and lowers the prices in foreign markets. Therefore, the producers and the government at home are better off, while the consumers are worse off, resulting in a total welfare loss. When the importing country is large enough, such an import policy results in lower world prices and gives rise to the optimal tariff policy. In the case of a domestic monopoly, tariffs and quotas yield similar welfare outcomes compared to the border restrictions in perfect competition, but they are non-equivalent because the quota lets the domestic monopoly keep its market power. The quota leads to higher domestic prices and a lower domestic output than the equivalent tariff. Thus, tariffs are preferred to quotas in the case of domestic monopoly.

When there is a foreign monopoly, the government's tariff policy reduces consumer surplus, and foreign exporters' net price decreases, resulting in a terms-of-trade gain for the home country. Therefore, the total welfare depends on the size of the terms-of-trade gains. Imperfect completion in international markets yields strategic trade policy that implies the government's role in policy design to protect their domestic sectors, such as tariffs and export subsidies.[28] The implementation of this policy has been a matter of debate for a long time. First of all, although import protection could be beneficial unliterally, it may worsen the world welfare in case of retaliation policies.[29] Secondly, some other factors, such as inefficient government intervention and limited distributive effects, can prevent trade gains.[30]

The idea that developing countries might benefit from protectionism, as indicated by the new trade theories, has received a certain criticism.[31] The main argument of these critiques states that imperfect competition is more dominant in developing country economies than in developed ones. Actually, the high concentration ratios in developing countries are an indication of such a market imperfection. The lack of antitrust policies and import substitution structures are other factors that harm trade. Additionally, the insufficiency of research and development expenditures on labor-intensive factors of production and raw materials may negatively impact the scale economies in developing countries.

In strategic agricultural trade, governments also play significant roles in controlling prices as state trading enterprises (STEs) through grain storage mechanisms. WTO lists the main issues related to the STEs as lack of transparency and possible negative trade effects.[32] The STEs can have many forms, such as statutory marketing boards, export marketing boards, regulatory marketing boards, fiscal monopolies, canalizing agencies, and foreign trade enterprises. According to the WTO, the STEs may be operated as a tool for certain trade policy instruments. These policy instruments, such as market access obligations, may be inconsistent with the provisions of the multilateral trading system. For instance, domestic markets can be protected through an STE by setting higher retail prices for imports. In some cases, the STEs can act as import protection instruments by reducing imports, negatively affecting exporters' welfare and influencing the terms of trade.[33] Alternatively, the STEs can provide a more stable food supply and price stability and, therefore, assure food security, especially in developing countries.[34] Given the fact that the STEs have different roles in developing countries and the level of development in terms of infrastructure, retailing, and finance varies by country and region, their roles need to be evaluated based on country-specific needs.

An increasing number of studies imply strategic trade policy, including for developing countries. Given the fact that strategic trade policy develops fast, it can integrate with the characteristics of developing countries and the formation of regional trading blocs.[35] For instance, developing countries' use of optimum tariffs must be accompanied by related industrial policies such as market entry.[36] In agricultural trade, the strategic trade policy may be relevant given the fact that processed products are gaining importance in world agricultural trade and limited firms are dominant.[37] Nevertheless, there should always be a precaution in designing such strategic policies such that these policies should be in line with the multilateral trading system and be backed by the regulatory institutions that deliver the possible positive outcomes of such policies to improve the distribution of income in a society.

Notes

1 Cemal Atici, "Weight perception and efficiency loss in bilateral trading: The case of US and EU agricultural policies," *Journal of Productivity Analysis*, 24(3), (2005a):283–292.

2 Alessandro Olper, et al., "Political reforms and public policy: Evidence from agricultural and food policies," *The World Bank Economic Review*, 28(1), (2014):21–47.

3 Rakhal Sarker, et al., "The political economy of systematic government intervention in agriculture," *Canadian Journal of Agricultural Economics*, 41(3), (1993):289–309.

4 Sabhan Asian, et al., "Sharing economy in organic food supply chains: A pathway to sustainable development," *International Journal of Production Economics*, 218, (2019):322–338.

5 Deborah Stone, *Policy Paradox, The Art of Political Decision Making* (New York: W.W.Norton&Company, 1997).

6 For a discussion on the subject in agricultural trade see Atici (2005b).

7 Avinash K. Dixit, Victor Norman, *Theory of International Trade* (Cambridge: Cambridge University Press, 1995).

8 Jaime de Melo, Sherman Robinson, "The impact of trade policies on income distribution in a planning model for Colombia," *Journal of Policy Modeling*, 2(1), (1980):81–100.

9 Peter H. Lindert, Jeffrey G. Williamson, "Does the Globalization Make the World More Unequal?" Working Paper 8228 (Cambridge: National Bureau of Economic Research, 2001).

10 Cemal Atici, P. Lynn Kennedy, "Tradeoffs between income distribution and welfare: The case of Turkey's integration into the European Union," *Journal of Policy Modeling*, 27(5), (2005c):553–563.

11 Hans Lofgren, "Trade reform and poor in Morocco. A rural-urban general equilibrium analysis of reduced protection," TMD Discussion Paper No: 38. (Washington, DC: International Food Policy Research Institute, 1999).

12 Klaus Salhofer, "Efficient income redistribution for a small country using optimal combined instruments," *Agricultural Economics*, 13, (1996):191–199.

13 John Baffes, Jacob Meerman, "From prices to incomes: Agricultural subsidization without protection?" *World Bank Research Observer*, 13(2), (1998):191–211.

14 Riham Shendy, "Efficiency gains from trade reform: Foreign input technology or import competition? Evidence from South Africa," *The International Trade Journal*, 26(5), (2012):385–412.

15 Stone, *Policy Paradox*, 61–107.

16 P.S. Ramakrishnan, "Increasing population and declining biological resources in the context of global change and globalization," *Journal of Biosciences*, 26(4), (2001):465–479.

17 Abishek Chaudhary, Thomas M. Brooks, "National consumption and global trade impacts on biodiversity," *World Development*, 121(2019):178–187.

18 Michael Flint, "Biological Diversity and Developing Countries," in A. Markandya, J. Richardson, eds, *Environmental Economics: A Reader*, (New York: St. Martin's Press, 1993):437–468.

19 Cemal Atici, "Liberalization-goals tradeoffs: Implications of agricultural trade liber-alization for developing countries," *Outlook on Agriculture*, 34(2), (2005b):83–89.
20 Paul R. Krugman, "Import Protection as Export Promotion. Inter-National Com-petition in the Presence of Oligopoly and Economies of Scale," in H. Kierkowski, ed, *Monopolistic Competition and International Trade*, (Oxford: Clarendon Press, 1984).
21 Elhanan Helpman, Paul R. Krugman, *Trade Policy and Market Structure* (Cam-bridge: The MIT Press, 1989).
22 For a detailed information see Robert E. Lucas, "On the mechanics of economic development," *Journal of Monetary Economics*, 22, (1988):3–42; Paul M. Romer, "The origins of endogenous growth," *Journal of Economic Perspectives*, 8(1), (1994):3–22.
23 Munisamy Gopinath, Terry L. Roe, "R&D spillovers: Evidence from U.S. food pro-cessing, farm machinery and agricultural sectors," *Economics of Innovation and New Technology*, 9(3), (2000):223–244.
24 Jorg Mayer, *Implications of New Trade and Endogenous Growth Theories for Diversification Policies of Commodity-Dependent Countries*. UNCTAD/OSG/DP/122.
25 Hans van Meijl, Frank van Tongeren, "Trade, technology spillovers, and food pro-duction in China," *Weltwirtschaftliches Archiv*, 134, (1998):423–449.
26 Matthew A. Cole, "Trade, the pollution haven hypothesis and the environmental Kuznets curve: Examining the linkages," *Ecological Economics*, 48(1), (2004):71–81.
27 For a detailed discussion on the imperfect competition and trade policy see Help-man and Krugman (1989) and Tweeten (1992).
28 For the seminal work on the issue see Brander and Spencer (1985).
29 Anming Zhang, Yimin Zhang, "An analysis of import protection as export promotion under economies of scale," *Japan and the World Economy*, 10(2), (1998):199–219.
30 Asad Alam, "The new trade theory and its relevance for developing countries," *The World Economy*, 18(3), (1995):367–385.
31 Ibid., 367–385.
32 See WTO (2023f).
33 Steve McCorriston, Donald MacLaren, "Assessing the distortionary impact of state trading in China," *Agricultural Economics*, 41(3–4), (2010):329–335.
34 For a discussion on the issue see Eugenio Díaz-Bonilla (2021).
35 Jing Linbo, "The development of the strategic trade policy and its application in China," *Chinese Economy*, 50(2), (2017):97–111.
36 Aditya Bhattacharjea, "Strategic tariffs and endogenous market structures: Trade and industrial policies under imperfect competition," *Journal of Development Eco-nomics*, 47(2), (1995):287–312.
37 Siemen Van Berkum, Hans Van Meijl, "The application of trade and growth theo-ries to agriculture: A survey," *The Australian Journal of Agricultural and Resource Economics*, 44(4), (2002):505–542.

References

Alam, A. (1995). The new trade theory and its relevance for developing countries. *The World Economy*, 18(3), 367–385.
Asian, S., Hafezalkotob, A., John, J.J. (2019). Sharing economy in organic food supply chains: A pathway to sustainable development. *International Journal of Production Economics*, 218, 322–338.
Atici, C. (2005a). Weight perception and efficiency loss in bilateral trading: The case of US and EU agricultural policies. *Journal of Productivity Analysis*, 24(3), 283–292.

Atici, C. (2005b). Liberalization-goals tradeoffs: Implications of agricultural trade liberalization for developing countries. *Outlook on Agriculture*, 34(2), 83–89.

Atici, C., Kennedy, P.L. (2005c). Tradeoffs between income distribution and welfare: The case of Turkey's integration into the European Union. *Journal of Policy Modeling*, 27(5), 553–563.

Baffes, J., Meerman, J. (1998). From prices to incomes: Agricultural subsidization without protection? *World Bank Research Observer*, 13(2), 191–211.

Berkum, S.V., Meijl, H.V. (2002). The application of trade and growth theories to agriculture: A survey. *The Australian Journal of Agricultural and Resource Economics*, 44(4), 505–542.

Bhattacharjea, A. (1995). Strategic tariffs and endogenous market structures: Trade and industrial policies under imperfect competition. *Journal of Development Economics*, 47(2), 287–312.

Brander, J.A., Spencer, B. (1985). Export subsidies and international market share rivalry. *Journal of International Economics*, 18(1–2), 83–100.

Chaudhary, A., Brooks, T.M. (2019). National consumption and global trade impacts on biodiversity. *World Development*, 121, 178–187.

Cole, M.A. (2004). Trade, the pollution haven hypothesis and the environmental Kuznets curve: Examining the linkages. *Ecological Economics*, 48(1), 71–81.

Diaz-Bonilla, E. (2021). Public Stockholdings, Special Safeguard Mechanism and State Trading Enterprises: What's Food Security Got to do with them, in V. Pinerio et al., eds. The road to the WTO twelfth Ministerial Conference: A Latin American and Caribbean perspective. https://ebrary.ifpri.org/utils/getfile/collection/p15738coll2/id/134771/filename/134978.pdf [Accessed September 20, 2023].

Dixit, A.K., Norman, V. (1995). *Theory of International Trade*. Cambridge: Cambridge University Press.

Flint, M. (1993). Biological Diversity and Developing Countries, in A. Markandya, J. Richardson, eds, *Environmental Economics: A Reader*. New York: St. Martin's Press, 437–468.

Gopinath, M., Roe, T.L. (2000). R&D spillovers: Evidence from U.S. food processing, farm machinery and agricultural sectors. *Economics of Innovation and New Technology*, 9(3), 223–244.

Helpman, E., Krugman, P.R. (1989). *Trade Policy and Market Structure*. Cambridge: The MIT Press.

Kierkowski, H. (Ed.) (1984). *Monopolistic Competition and International Trade*. Oxford: Clarendon Press.

Krugman, P. (1984). Import Protection as Export Promotion. Inter-National Competition in the Presence of Oligopoly and Economies of Scale, in H. Kierkowski, ed, *Monopolistic Competition and International Trade*. Oxford: Clarendon Press.

Linbo, J. (2017). The development of the strategic trade policy and its application in China. *Chinese Economy*, 50(2), 97–111.

Lindert, P.H., Williamson, J.G. (2001). Does the Globalization Make the World More Unequal? Working Paper 8228. Cambridge: National Bureau of Economic Research.

Lofgren, H. (1999). Trade reform and poor in Morocco. A rural-urban general equilibrium analysis of reduced protection. TMD Discussion Paper No: 38. Washington, DC: International Food Policy Research Institute.

Lucas, R.E. (1988). On the mechanics of economic development. *Journal of Monetary Economics*, 22, 3–42.

Mayer, J. (1996). Implications of New Trade and Endogenous Growth Theories for Diversification Policies of Commodity-Dependent Countries. UNCTAD/OSG/DP/122.

McCorriston, S., MacLaren, D. (2010). Assessing the distortionary impact of state trading in China. *Agricultural Economics*, 41(3–4), 329–335.

van Meijl, H., Tongeren, F. (1998). Trade, technology spillovers, and food production in China. *Weltwirtschaftliches Archiv*, 134, 423–449.

de Melo, J., Robinson, S. (1980). The impact of trade policies on income distribution in a planning model for Colombia. *Journal of Policy Modeling*, 2(1), 81–100.

Olper, A., Fałkowski, J., Swinnen, J. (2014). Political reforms and public policy: Evidence from agricultural and food policies. *The World Bank Economic Review*, 28(1), 21–47.

Ramakrishnan, P.S. (2001), Increasing population and declining biological resources in the context of global change and globalization. *Journal of Biosciences*, 26(4), 465–479.

Romer, P.M. (1994). The origins of endogenous growth. *Journal of Economic Perspectives*, 8(1), 3–22.

Salhofer, K. (1996). Efficient income redistribution for a small country using optimal combined instruments. *Agricultural Economics*, 13, 191–199.

Sarker, R., Meilke, K., Hoy, M. (1993). The political economy of systematic government intervention in agriculture. *Canadian Journal of Agricultural Economics*, 41(3), 289–309.

Shendy, R. (2012). Efficiency gains from trade reform: Foreign input technology or import competition? Evidence from South Africa. *The International Trade Journal*, 26(5), 385–412.

Stone, D. (1997). *Policy Paradox. The Art of Political Decision Making.* New York: W.W. Norton & Company.

Tweeten, L. (1992). *Agricultural Trade. Principles and Policies.* Boulder, CO: Westview Press.

WTO (2023). Technical Information on State Trading Enterprises. https://www.wto.org/english/tratop_e/statra_e/statra_info_e.htm [Accessed September 21, 2023].

Zhang, A., Zhang, Y. (1998). An analysis of import protection as export promotion under economies of scale. *Japan and the World Economy*, 10(2), 199–219.

Part III
Dynamics of Sustainable Food Trade

6   A Framework for the Sustainable Food Policies and Trade

This section mainly examines the interaction between sustainable development and food trade. Although in a conventional case, trade interacts mainly with food safety and food security, nowadays, in a broader sense, trade interacts with many other variables. There are mainly seven factors that shape sustainable development polices in agriculture. These are production, consumption, value chains, trade, social aspects, ecology and environment, and international context. Therefore, examining and discussing these drivers' interactions with sustainable policy formulation is necessary.

On the production side, using environmentally friendly inputs and good agricultural practices to protect the land and other related resources are necessary conditions for sustainable development in agriculture. On the other hand, ensuring food safety, security, and sustainable consumption is required for successful sustainable food policies. In the globalized world, sustainable development policies interact with certain global factors such as foreign direct investment (FDI), energy needs, and international climate change provisions such as flexibility mechanisms. As the agricultural sector grows in an economy, the energy need becomes a major issue, especially for countries that depend on imports. Producing renewable energy not only decreases dependency on import but also alleviates environmental problems. However, these types of energy projects need a careful project evaluation to prevent some unseen side effects, such as the impact on human health and the quality of agricultural commodities produced. In that case, the tradeoff between providing renewable energy for the production side and the environmental impacts on the stakeholders involved requires a participatory approach. These issues are examined in detail in the following sections. Figure 6.1 presents a possible interaction of sustainable food policies.

DOI: 10.4324/9781032708577-4

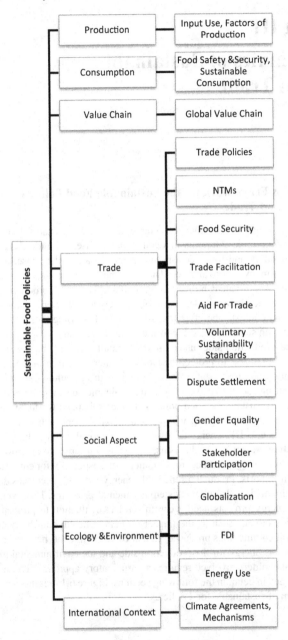

Figure 6.1 Key Determinants of Sustainable Food Policies and Trade

7   Non-Tariff Measures and Food Trade

Non-tariff measures (NTMs) are gaining importance as trade policy tools in line with rising global trade flows. NTMs have a high share in overall trade restrictiveness, and in some estimates, NTMs are more trade restrictive than tariffs.[1] NTMs account for almost four times as much as tariffs in the overall trade restrictiveness index (OTRI) faced by low-income countries' exports. In addition, the share of NTMs in OTRI is high in the agricultural sector compared to the manufacturing sector in all exporters.[2]

The NTMs broadly cover three sections: technical measures, non-technical measures, and export measures. The list of NTMs classified by UNCTAD[3] can be seen in Table 7.1.

Sanitary and phytosanitary measures (SPS) refer to policies that are applied to protect human or animal life from risks arising from additives, contaminants, toxins, or disease-causing organisms in their food and to protect biodiversity. In addition, geographic restrictions, systems approach, registration, tolerance limits, labeling, certification, and hygienic requirements are classified in such measures. The systems approach covers at least two measures that are independent of each other to achieve SPS management. Implementing a systems approach can improve export performances or replace more restrictive measures like prohibition.[4] Technical barriers to trade (TBT) refer to technical regulations and procedures for assessing conformity with technical regulations and standards, excluding measures covered by the SPS Agreement. It also includes authorization, registration, tolerance limits, labeling, product identity, certification, and origin.

Contingent trade protective measures cover the policies implemented to counteract particular adverse effects of imports in the importing country's market, including measures aimed at unfair foreign trade practices contingent upon the fulfillment of certain procedural and substantive requirements. These measures include antidumping, countervailing investigation, and safeguard measures. Non-automatic licensing, quotas, prohibitions, and quantity control measures other than SPS and TBT measures refer to control measures generally aimed at restraining the quantity of goods that can be imported, regardless of whether they come from different sources or one specific supplier. These measures include seasonal quotas, tariff rate quotas, and voluntary export restrictions. Price control measures, including additional taxes and charges, are related to the measures implemented to control or affect the prices of imported goods in order to support the domestic price of certain products when the import prices of these goods are lower; to insulate price fluctuation in domestic markets, or price instability in a foreign market; and to increase or preserve tax revenue. They cover variable levies, custom surcharges, seasonal duties, and consumption taxes. Finance measures are intended to regulate the access to and cost of foreign exchange for imports and define the terms of payment. They may increase import costs in the same manner as tariff measures.

Table 7.1 Non-Tariff Measures

Imports	Coverage
I-Technical Measures	
1-Sanitary and Phytosanitary Measures	Measures related to protection of human or animal life from risks arising from additives, contaminants, toxins, or disease-causing organisms in their food and to protection of biodiversity. Geographic restrictions, systems approach, registration, tolerance limits, labeling, certification, and hygienic requirements.
2-Technical Barriers to Trade	Measures related to technical regulations and procedures for assessment of conformity with technical regulations and standards, excluding measures covered by the SPS Agreement. Authorization, registration, tolerance limits, labeling, product identity, certification, origin.
3-Pre-Shipment Inspection and Other Formalities	Inspection and direct consignment (without third country).
II. Non-Technical Measures	
1-Contingent Trade Protective Measures	Measures implemented to counteract particular adverse effects of imports in the market of the importing country, such as measures aimed at unfair foreign trade practices. Antidumping, countervailing investigation, and safeguard measure.
2-Non-Automatic Licensing, Quotas, Prohibitions, and Quantity Control Measures other than SPS and TBT measures	Control measures aimed at restraining the quantity of goods imported, regardless of the source or a specific supplier. Seasonal quotas, tariff rate quotas, and voluntary export restrictions.
3-Price Control Measures including Additional Taxes and Charges	Measures implemented to control or affect the prices of imported goods in order to support the domestic price of certain products in situations when the import prices of these goods are lower; to insulate price fluctuation in domestic markets, or price instability in a foreign market; and to increase or preserve tax revenue. Variable levies, custom surcharges, seasonal duties, and consumption taxes.
4-Finance Measures	Finance measures are intended to regulate the access to and cost of foreign exchange for imports and define the terms of payment. They may increase import costs in the same manner as tariff measures. Advanced payment requirements, deposits, multiple exchange rates, and bank authorization.

5-Measures Affecting competition	Measures to grant exclusive or special preferences or privileges to one or more limited groups of economic operators. State trading enterprises and compulsory use of national services.
6-Trade-Related Investment Measures	Local content measures and trade balancing measures.
7-Distribution Restrictions	Distribution of goods inside the importing country may be restricted. It may be controlled through additional license or certification requirements. Geographical restrictions.
8-Restrictions on Post-Sales Services	Measures restricting producers of exported goods to provide post-sales service in the importing country.
9-Subsidies (Excluding Export)	Financial contribution by a government or public body, grant, loan, equity infusion, guarantee, income, or price support, which confers a benefit and is specific.
10- Government Procurement Restrictions	Measures that control the purchase of goods by government agencies, generally by preferring national providers.
11-Intellectual Property	Measures related to intellectual property rights in trade, patents, trademarks, industrial designs, layout designs of integrated circuits, copyright, geographical indications, and trade secrets.
12-Rules of Origin	Rules of origin refer to laws, regulations, and administrative determinations of general application applied by the government of importing countries to determine the country of origin of goods. These measures are especially important in implementing trade policy instruments such as antidumping and countervailing duties, origin marking, and safeguard measures.
Exports Export Related Measures	Export-related measures are measures applied by the government of the exporting country on exported goods. Licenses, quotas, state trading enterprises, export subsidies.

Source: Compiled from UNCTAD, 2019.

These measures include advanced payment requirements, deposits, multiple exchange rates, and bank authorization. Measures affecting competition refer to the measures granting exclusive or special preferences or privileges to one or more limited groups of economic operators. Such measures include trading enterprises and compulsory use of national services.

Trade-related investment measures refer to local content measures and trade balancing measures. Distribution restrictions cover the limitations on the distribution of goods inside the importing country. It may be controlled through additional license or certification requirements and may include geographical restrictions. Restrictions on post-sales service measures are related to regulations such as restricting producers of exported goods from providing post-sales service in the importing country. Subsidies are a financial contribution by a government or public body, grant, loan, equity infusion, guarantee, income, or price support, which confers a benefit and is specific. Government procurement restrictions refer to measures controlling the purchase of goods by government agencies, generally by preferring national providers. Intellectual property measures are related to intellectual property rights in trade, patents, trademarks, industrial designs, layout designs of integrated circuits, copyrights, geographical indications (GIs), and trade secrets. Rules of origin refer to the laws, regulations, and administrative determinations of general application applied by the government of importing countries to determine the country of origin of goods. Rules of origin are particularly important in implementing trade policy instruments such as antidumping and countervailing duties, origin marking, and safeguard measures. Export-related measures refer to the policies applied by the government of the exporting country on exported goods, such as licenses, quotas, state trading enterprises, and export subsidies.

There are limited studies examining the equivalence of NTMs in agricultural commodities. In one of the sector-specific studies examining the prevalence of price-based ad valorem equivalent of NTMs utilizing multicountry bilateral trade,[5] it was found that the lowest total NTMs are in wheat, followed by plant-based fibers, and the highest NTMs are in sugar cane/beet, followed by other cereals and other meat products. In addition, there is some evidence that rules of origin policies are important barriers to trade flow.[6]

When NTM usage by the development status is examined, it has been observed that the frequency index (presence or absence of an NTM) and coverage ratio (share of trade subject to NTM), prevalence score (number of NTMs applied to a given product), and regulatory intensity (adjusted differences in regulations) vary by the level of development. According to the UNCTAD report,[7] the NTMs in developed countries affect a higher share of products and trade than those in developing countries. In least developed countries (LDCs), around 40% of imports are subject to the NTMs, while in developed countries, this value is around 80%. Another important finding of the report indicates that the NTMs affect more products and are more pervasive in developed countries. Developed countries utilize more types of NTMs than developing countries for a given product. In addition, the regulatory intensity indicates that developed countries have a higher intensity of regulation. In terms of the export side, LDCs utilize the NTMs more frequently.

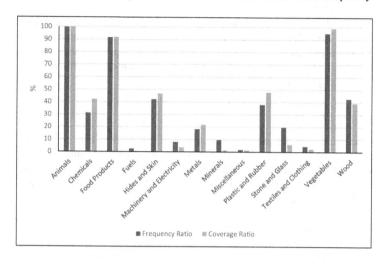

Figure 7.1 The EU's SPS Frequency and Coverage Ratios by Sector
Source: World Bank-WITS, 2022a.

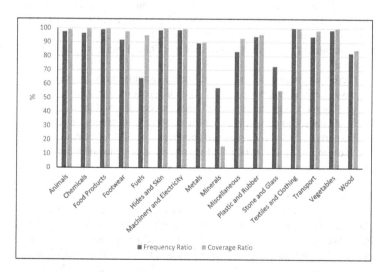

Figure 7.2 The EU's TBT Frequency and Coverage Ratios by Sector
Source: World Bank-WITS, 2022a.

Although these measures cover only 20% of their export products, they account for around half of their export value.[8] As an example of SPS measures in agriculture, Figure 7.1 presents the prevalence of SPS measures for the EU by sector.

According to the figure, animal products, vegetable products, and food products have high shares of frequency and coverage ratios in the context of the SPS measures in the EU. On the other hand, the frequency and coverage ratios by TBT are presented in Figure 7.2. According to that figure, most sectors are subject to the TBT measures.

7.1   *Food Safety*

Food safety policies are an essential part of the NTMs. This issue is especially critical for developing country exports. These measures cover all stages of the food chain, such as feed production, food processing, storage, transport, and retailing.[9] The Agreement on the Application of Sanitary and Phytosanitary Measures (the SPS Agreement)[10] is an international treaty of the World Trade Organization (WTO). The Agreement was negotiated during the Uruguay Round and entered into force with the establishment of the WTO in 1995. Food safety standards are part of NTMs and currently are the most relevant ones in the context of trade interactions between developed and developing countries. These safety measures always have the potential to be barriers, especially for developing countries, at least in the short and medium run, if exporters from developing countries cannot comply with them in a timely manner. Table 7.2 presents an overview of major food safety standards. It must be underlined that there is no homogeneity of the standards, although there are specific (Codex) guidelines and general standards.

There are certain concerns for food safety recently raised by various parties involved in international trade.[11] The main reason is that the SPS issues are gaining more importance as tariff barriers decrease, and there are certain levels of concern in developing countries that these measures are preventing their exports to markets of developed countries. The SPS Agreement indicates that measures must either be based on scientific evidence of risk or recognized international standards. On the other hand, member countries are free to set their standards, provided that they are based on science. The Agreement indicates that the SPS measures should be based on recognized international standards, specifically those of the FAO/WHO Codex Alimentarius Commission, the World Organization for Animal Health (WOAH), the International Plant Protection Convention (IPPC), science, including scientific assessment of risk. This temporary precautionary principle favors the safety-first approach in the absence of international standards or scientific evidence. The most common complaints are related to non-compliance with international standards by importers, and long delays in completing risk assessments are frequent complaints.[12]

Table 7.2 Major Food Safety Standards and Guidelines

Type	Main Commodities Affected	Related International Regulation/Guidelines
I – Food and Feed Safety		
I-1. Contaminants		
-Aflatoxins	Dried fruits and nuts	Codex Alimentarius, 1995–2019
-MRLs	Tea, Fruits, and Vegetables	Codex Alimentarius, 1995–2019 OECD, 2008
-Others (Other contaminants, metals in food)	Fish	Codex Alimentarius, 1995–2019
I.2. Genetically Modified Organisms	Linseeds, Rice, Maize, Soybean, Papaya, and Canola	Cartagena Protocol, 2000 Codex Annex II, 2003
-GMO Content		WTO SPS, 1995
-Risk Assessments		OECD Task Force and Working Groups
-LLP		
II - Animal Health	Animal products	WTO, Codex, WOAH
-Health Certificates		
III - Plant Health	Plant Products	WTO, Codex, IPPC
-Plant Certificates		
IV - Biological	Animal Products	The Tripartite Zoonoses Guide
-Zoonotic		(FAO, WHO, WOAH), 2019
V- Environmental	Food Products	Rotterdam Convention, 1998
V.1. Chemicals in Food Products		Cartagena Protocol, 2000
V.2. Biodiversity impacts of novel food and feed		

In food trade, food safety regulations usually have three main effects: the trade-impeding effect, the neutral effect, and the catalyst effect. The trade-impeding effect occurs due to the trade-distorting impact of regulations. This effect mainly harms the export performances of developing countries. The neutral effect is primarily observed in developed exporting countries, where they can comply with restrictive regulations. The main reasons for this effect are high research and development expenditures and a high level of standards.

Furthermore, when regulations force exporting countries to invest more in a specific market and increase their share in world trade, it leads to the catalyst effect. This effect also occurs when developed countries replace the exports of negatively affected developing countries in world markets. The main dynamics of the catalyst effect can be classified as research and development (R&D), scale effect, institutional effect, and efforts for harmonization. It is a known fact that most of the R&D is observed in the economies of developed countries. However, the scale effect can be observed in emerging markets, where firm size is increased to comply with restrictive regulations. Alternatively, the institutional effect includes institutional governance and guidance to provide domestic exporting firms with market information and technical assistance. The harmonization effect is observed when a candidate country aims to join an economic union and harmonizes its regulations according to the principles of the union.[13]

The impact of food safety regulations on trade performance varies by country and commodity. In addition, meeting the strict regulations requires a period, namely an adjustment process. The research on the issue provides a certain level of evidence for the discussion. For instance, food safety standards imposed by importing countries had a negative effect on China's agricultural exports.[14] Similarly, it was found that developed countries' food safety standards had a deterring impact on the processed food exports of developing countries.[15] However, as an example of the catalyst effect, Senegal's vegetable exports grew significantly after food safety standards were adopted due to a shift of production from smallholders to large-scale production.[16] The HACCP standards implemented by the US have a negative impact on developing countries but a positive impact on developed countries for US seafood imports.[17] In addition, there is a certain level of evidence demonstrating that some countries are utilizing high-quality and safety standards to reposition themselves in competitive global markets.[18] The impact of food safety standards also varies depending on the commodity in question. For instance, harmonizing the EU food safety regulation in 2002 positively influenced hazelnut exports, while the EU food safety regulation in 2007 reduced the volume of fig exports. The rise in export unit values demonstrates that Turkish primary food products responded to the EU food safety regulation with quality improvements accompanied by higher unit prices.[19]

The stringent standards may cause an adjustment period for the exporters. Meeting stringent standards primarily increases the fixed cost for the export destination; however, when firms adjust their production to comply with the standards, the standards do not impact the intensity of exports.[20] Implementing food safety regulations has also been a matter of dispute in international trade forums. The long duration of the process and the lack of regional representation highlight the importance of empowering the capacity of developing countries in terms of legal aspects such as WTO's Dispute Settlement Mechanism.[21]

The findings indicate that standards can stimulate developing countries' food exports; however, capacity development and an adjustment period are required for export performances. Although the adjustment to the strict regulations may increase the cost reflected in commodity prices, in the long run, the process can improve the trade performances and the overall well-being of producers and exporters. At this stage, public-private partnership is essential in the adoption of innovations by producers and firms towards the implementation of standards and relevant technologies.

7.2   Biotechnology and Food Trade

Biotechnology refers to a variety of technologies that can be applied for a range of different purposes, including the genetic improvement of plant varieties and animal populations to increase their yields or efficiency, genetic characterization and conservation of genetic resources, plant or animal disease diagnosis, vaccine development, and improvement of feeds.[22] Genetically modified organisms (GMOs) are one of the biotechnology applications and refer to an organism that has been transformed by the insertion of one or more transgenes.[23] The increasing cultivation of genetically modified (GM) crops has raised many concerns, such as food safety, environmental effects, and socioeconomic issues. The total area of GM crops amounted to 190 million hectares in 2019, and the main crops planted are soybeans, maize, cotton, canola, sugar beet, alfa, and papaya.[24] The main concerns are related to the possible toxicity and allergenicity of GM foods and products. Certain concerns about environmental risks include the impact of introgression of the transgenes into the natural landscape, the impact of gene flow, the effect on non-target organisms, the evolution of pest resistance, and the loss of biodiversity. The social and ethical concerns include restricting access to genetic resources, loss of traditions, such as saving seeds, private sector monopoly, and loss of income of resource-poor farmers.[25]

On the other hand, the low-level presence (LLP) and adventitious presence (AP) of GMOs in internationally traded food crops have been a major issue recently. GM food crop production is increasing in developed and developing countries. Many countries have quite diverse GMO regulations. Asynchronous approvals (AA) and zero tolerance policy have been reported to have trade diversion effects by some exporters.[26]

7.2.1   Case Study: Biotechnology and Food Trade

A Food and Agriculture Organization (FAO) survey conducted in 2014[27] revealed that half of the respondents produce GM crops for research or commercial use. In the study, 78% of respondents indicated that they have a GMO regulation; however, 22% either do not have or are planning to have regulations in the future. This situation may cause uncontrolled import of GM crops, especially for developing countries. Technical capacity is quite an important factor for detecting GMOs; however, only 33% of the respondents indicated that they have a technical capacity to detect GMOs in imports. The survey also found that 37% of the respondents faced LLP/AP in their imports in the last ten years. The main crops that are subject to LLP/AP incidents are linseed, rice, maize, and soybean. The US, China, and Canada were the main exporters whose consignments were involved in LLP/AP incidents in the survey.

The findings reveal that the major factors contributing to the trade risk are different policies on GMOs existing between trading partners, unintentional movement of GM crops, and different timing for approvals. The LLP/AP incidents reported by the importing countries are usually handled through rejection or market withdrawals by the importers of developed countries, and in some cases, it was accepted by some developing countries. These incidents have several welfare implications. The incidents can lead to income loss for exporters and producers. The economic analysis based on the survey and bilateral trade data revealed that food safety regulations faced by exporters have a certain level of deterrent effect on food trade.

Moreover, consumers in importing countries can potentially face higher domestic prices when the import is deterred from one country and directed to a trading partner. In that context, it is essential that GM crop-producing countries take all the necessary measures in the stages of production, harvesting, transportation, storage, and marketing to eliminate the low presence in conventional crops. Evidently, more international collaboration is needed in this area. It should be kept in mind that when evaluating the impacts of related regulations and standards, a comprehensive approach that covers consumer safety and environmental effects should be considered together with the economic effects.[28]

7.3   *Technical Barriers to Trade and Agriculture*

TBT refers to measures related to the technical regulations, procedures, standards, labeling, and rules of origin in international trade. The TBT Agreement aims to ensure that the regulations, standards, and procedures are non-discriminatory and do not form unnecessary obstacles to trade.[29] These barriers sometimes lead to disputes among the WTO members when importing partners aim to protect their producers or consumers. The stringency of TBTs can significantly reduce the agricultural exports of developing countries to developed ones.[30] On the other hand, the consumer may be willing to pay a premium for a food labeling system that certifies working conditions in producing the related commodity.[31] Variations in certification systems and a high number of certifying institutions in food products worldwide, such as Fairtrade, can lead to misinformation for consumers and governments.[32] Therefore, international collaboration in certification standards is needed. Some of the recently selected TBT disputes in agriculture, according to the WTO, are presented in Table 7.3.

7.4   *Trade-Related Intellectual Property Rights (TRIPS) and Food Trade*

Intellectual property rights refer to copyrights and industrial property such as trademarks, patents, and GIs.[33] The WTO's TRIPS Agreement has introduced the rules related to intellectual properties (IP) into the multilateral trading system and covers areas such as minimum standards of protection, procedures for enforcement, dispute settlement, and implementation procedures. The Agreement sets minimum IP protection standards for member countries' legislation. In addition, with this Agreement, developed countries are required to provide incentives to their institutions for technology transfer and technical cooperation to LDCs in the areas of laws, regulations, and training.

Table 7.3 Some Selected WTO Cases Citing TBT for Consultation in Agriculture

Case	Year	Complainant	Respondent
Certain Measures Concerning Palm Oil and Oil Palm Crop-Based Biofuels	2021	Malaysia	EU
Certain Measures Concerning Palm Oil and Oil Palm Crop-Based Biofuels	2019	Indonesia	EU
Measures Concerning the Importation of Bovine Meat	2016	Brazil	EU
Measures Concerning the Importation of Chicken Meat and Chicken Products	2014	Brazil	Indonesia
Certain Measures on the Importation and Marketing of Biodiesel and Measures Supporting the Biodiesel Industry	2013	Argentina	EU
Measures Prohibiting the Importation and Marketing of Seal Products	2009	Norway	EU

Source: Compiled from WTO, 2022b.

The impact of TRIPS on trade flow varies. For instance, in one of the studies, developing countries' agricultural trade is negatively affected by IPR regulations.[34] In terms of GIs, the protection of GIs creates trade when the importing and exporting countries have GI-protected products, but a trade-diverting effect occurs when the importing country does not have GIs.[35] GIs can improve welfare, but they can also be a protectionist instrument. The political and economic factors may lead to these types of regulations as an alternative to conventional trade policies.[36] Another issue is the efficiency of the current intellectual protection regime, which includes financing and organizing innovations. A well-functioning patent system requires careful attention, such as the number of patents, open-source systems, and publicly financed innovations.[37] Related reforms in the intellectual protection system can benefit both developed and developing countries to achieve their sustainable development goals. Given that there are limited studies examining the TRIPs on the food trade and sustainable development, further research examining the linkages certainly will help better understand the issue and formulate sustainable policies.

As mentioned before, regulation through NTMs varies by the level of development. In another related report of the WTO covering agrifood products and NTMs,[38] it is demonstrated that developed countries regulate 75% of the imported products, followed by LDCs (60%) and by developing countries (50%) through NTMs. These measures affect around 80% of global trade for developing countries and LDCs, followed by 70% of the developing countries. On average, developing countries and LDCs have two and three NTMs, and developed countries have four NTMs on average for each traded product. Across the countries, agrifood products are the most regulated, such that around 90–100% of the imported products are affected by the NTMs. In addition, developed countries regulate agricultural imports more intensively than developing countries based on the prevalence scores. In terms of coverage ratio by type, TBT measures rank first (70%), followed by quantity controls, export controls, price controls, and SPS measures.

Based on the data, developed countries utilize NTMs more frequently and intensively than developing countries, and the share of NTMs is quite high in agricultural commodities. Given the fact that agricultural exports account for a significant share in LDCs and developing countries' total exports, NTMs implemented by developed countries impede trade flow. This, in return, has a negative impact on developing countries' trade balance and overall welfare. The lack of developing countries' participation in setting international measures such as SPS and strict regulations that impede trade for some developing countries are some of the major challenges in multilateral trade negotiations.

8 Food Security

Food security refers to accessing sufficient, safe, and nutritious food.[39] In that context, the four main dimensions of food security are food availability, access, utilization, and stability.[40] According to a recent report,[41] the prevalence of undernourishment is around 9.8%, and people facing hunger are 8% of the world population, while almost 3.1 billion people cannot afford a healthy diet. Food loss and food waste are two other issues in food security. Globally, 14% of food is lost during the harvest, and 17% is wasted at the retail and consumption stages.[42]

Certain food security indicators are presented in Figure 8.1. The figure shows the cereal import dependency ratio. The ratio indicates the level of dependence on cereal import, and a higher ratio means higher dependence. As seen, the dependency ratio is high in Africa and lowest in Oceania. In addition, there is a slightly increasing trend in the region of Africa.

The prevalence of moderate or severe food insecurity in the total population is presented in Figure 8.2. According to the figure, food insecurity is quite high in Africa (60%), followed by the region of Latin America and the Caribbean.

Achieving food security requires the successful implementation of food and macroeconomic policies ranging from enhancing food supply, investment, adaptation to and mitigation of climate change, and multilateral collaboration, including food aid and trade. The role of trade in food security and sustainability is inevitable. Trade allows countries to access an adequate amount of food at the lowest possible cost and helps reduce emissions through the efficient use of natural resources.[43] Although conventional trade theories advocate specialization in production and trade, recent evidence suggests alternative approaches. Concentrating on production may decrease food supply, and promoting diversification in food production reduces the risk of food

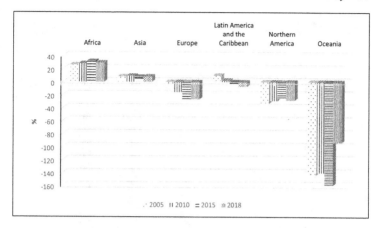

Figure 8.1 Cereal Import Dependency Ratio-2005–2018.

Source: FAOSTAT, 2023.

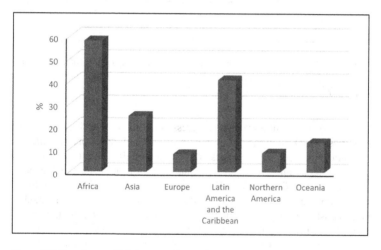

Figure 8.2 Prevalence of Moderate or Severe Food Insecurity in the Total Population, %, 2021.

Source: FAOSTAT, 2023.

deficit.[44] In addition, concentration on production rather than diversification may harm sustainability. On the other hand, the import of agricultural commodities, especially from distant partners, may lead to high emission levels due to transportation.[45] A predictable trading system can play an essential role in global food security by constructing an international food system that is more efficient and responsive to world supply shocks.[46]

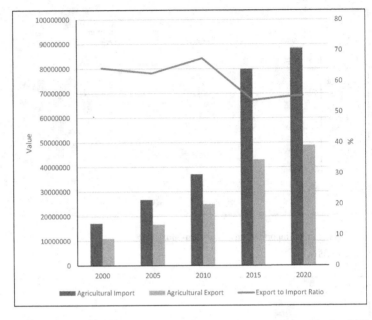

Figure 8.3 Net Food Importing Developing Countries' Trade Values, 1000 USD, 2000 2020.

Source: FAOSTAT, 2023.

Another important issue is the progress of net food-importing developing countries (NFIDCs) in the global trading system. Figure 8.3 presents the agricultural export and import values in five-year periods. The data indicate that the agricultural imports of the NFIDCs have increased more than their export, and the gap is widening. Actually, the export-to-import ratio in agricultural commodities decreased to 55% in 2020 from 64% in 2000. Undoubtedly, given constraints such as population growth and climate change, their trade performance needs special attention in the context of food security.

A framework for achieving food security with trade in a sustainable manner is demonstrated in Figure 8.4.

Price changes through trade have some implications for food security. In theory, an increase in food prices and price spikes benefits the net food exporters while harming the consumers in net food importers. Actually, in most food-exporting developing countries, these price spikes also harm domestic consumers due to low income. Secondly, most of the time, these price spikes are not transferred to the producers because of the structure of the markets and inefficient producer organizations. An increase in export revenue has different impacts on the factors of production and can benefit specific groups, such as skilled labor and business owners in trade-intensive sectors, deteriorating

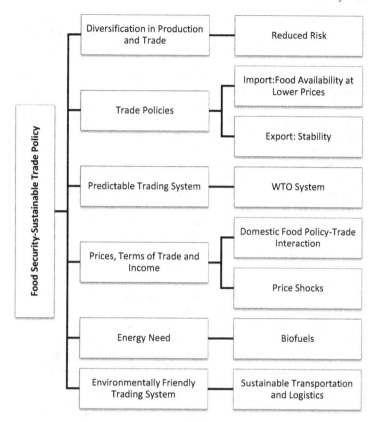

Figure 8.4 Food Security-Sustainable Trade Interaction

the distribution of income. Transferring trade gains to low-income consumers and, therefore, strengthening the purchasing power require a comprehensive domestic-trade policy interaction covering support schemes, poverty alleviation, and efficient income distribution policies.[47] Developed countries' agricultural policies, such as subsidies, may lead to adverse effects on the economies of developing countries through lower food prices. Although lower food prices may lower the risk of food insecurity, in the long run, such policies negatively impact the producers and consumers in developing countries, especially those exporting agricultural commodities. Certainly, this issue is complex and requires global efforts in the multilateral trading system.

An important concept, terms of trade, can play a major role in food security. If export-oriented growth improves the export prices relative to the import prices, an increase in terms of trade improves a country's welfare. However, sometimes the terms of trade deteriorate severely, for instance, due to a high level of competition in world markets. In that case, a country is made worse off by growth called immiserizing growth. This phenomenon may explain certain agricultural growth and food insecurity issues for some developing countries.[48] Another issue to consider is that an increase in trade flow in tandem with globalization does not lead to similar consequences for the whole country groups. Although the WTO and subsequent reforms aim to liberalize trade, these efforts do not lead to the intended results, especially for developing countries, due to technical and capacity development-related issues. Recent findings indicate that although the share of developing countries in agricultural exports increased, in terms of total exports, developed countries improved their shares substantially, and the gap in terms of value is widening. The findings underline the necessity of more active participation by developing countries in trade negotiations and technical and capacity support for trade facilitation.[49]

As the world population and energy demand increase, alternative energy resources are being utilized in response to meet the demand. Biofuels produced from food grains and oilseeds are considered alternative energy resources. However, biofuel production affects internationally traded food prices, especially in developed countries,[50] leading to food insecurity in developing countries. For certain, the issue needs to be addressed in the Development Agenda of the WTO negotiations. Price volatility in international food commodities has adverse effects on food security. Many reasons, such as climate change, supply shocks, restrictive trade policies, and speculations in futures markets, cause volatility. For instance, a study examining the speculation-futures commodity markets interaction[51] found that short-run speculations in agricultural commodity markets lead to price volatility. There are a few methods to reduce price volatility, such as active involvement in international marketing information systems, regulations of agricultural derivative markets, participating and negotiating in the multilateral trading system, revising biofuel policies, establishing safety nets for the vulnerable in the population, and developing risk management instruments to mitigate the impact of the price shocks.[52]

9   Trade Facilitation and Agriculture

Trade costs cover policy barriers, both tariffs and non-tariff barriers, transportation costs, communication and information costs, exchange rate costs, and legal and regulatory costs. Since these costs are impediments to trade, WTO's trade facilitation efforts aim to reduce trade-related costs. Trade facilitation refers to facilitating, simplifying, modernizing, and harmonizing export and import procedures. The Trade Facilitation Agreement (TFA) entered into force in 2017 and covered measures for effective cooperation, capacity building, and technical assistance.[53] The WTO estimates that[54] the full implementation of the agreement could reduce trade costs by 14.3% and boost global trade by around 1 trillion USD per year. The contents of the TFA are summarized in Table 9.1.

Table 9.1 WTO's Trade Facilitation Agreement Measures

Measure	Coverage
Publication	WTO members must publish trade-related information in a non-discriminatory and easily accessible manner.
Information available through internet	Members are required to make practical guidelines for trade and appeal procedures available on the internet, related forms, and contact details of enquiry points.
Enquiry points	Members are required to establish enquiry points to answer trade-related queries within a reasonable time.
Notification	Members are required to notify the official places and contact information related to publication, information through the internet, and enquiry points.
Comments and information before entry into force	Traders and other interested parties must be given an opportunity and reasonable time to comment on new proposals or amended legal acts. In addition, new or amended laws and regulations must be made publicly available before their entry into force.
Consultations	Border agencies must hold regular consultations with traders and stakeholders.
Advance rulings	Before the import of goods, customs authorities must issue written decisions about certain admissible customs disciplines to the applicants upon request.
Procedures for appeal or review	Members must provide traders with the right to appeal decisions made by customs in an administrative or judicial proceeding.
Notifications for enhanced controls or inspections	When designing a system of notification for enhanced inspection of food products, members must abide by the principles of transparency, scientific evidence, and risk-based inspection.
Detention	Members must promptly notify an importer or carrier when imported goods are being held for inspection.
Test procedures	Members may grant, upon request, an opportunity for a second confirmatory test in case of an adverse finding.
General disciplines on fees and charges	Members are required to publish import and export fees and charges transparently.
Specific disciplines on fees and charges	Fees and charges for customs processing must be limited in amount to the approximate cost of the services rendered.
Penalty disciplines	Penalties imposed for legal, administrative, or procedural requirements must be based on facts and must be commensurate with the degree and severity of the breach.
Pre-arrival processing	Members must allow for the submission of documents and information before the arrival in order to facilitate the processing and release of goods.
Electronic payment	Members should allow electronic payment of duties, taxes, fees, and charges.
Separation of release	Members must adopt procedures allowing the release of goods before the final determination of custom charges, provided that related requirements are met.
Risk management	Members must establish a risk management system for customs control.

(*Continued*)

Table 9.1 (Continued)

Measure	Coverage
Post-clearance audit	Members must use post-clearance audits with a view to expediting the release of goods.
Average release times	Members are encouraged to measure and publish the average release time in a consistent manner.
Authorized operators	Members must provide certain additional trade facilitation benefits to authorized operators who meet specified criteria.
Expedited shipments	Members must establish special procedures to expedite the release of goods entered through air cargo facilities.
Perishable goods	Members must provide priority treatment for perishable goods to prevent their deterioration at the border.
Border Agency Cooperation	Border authorities and agencies must cooperate and coordinate border controls and procedures in order to facilitate trade.
Movement of goods	Members must allow the transportation of imported goods from the point of entry to an inland customs office, where the goods would be released or cleared.
Formalities	Members must examine formalities and documentation requirements on a regular basis in order to minimize and reduce them.
Acceptance of copies	Border agencies must accept copies of supporting documents that may be required for trade formalities.
Use of international standards	Members are encouraged to use relevant international standards as a basis for their import, export, and transit formalities and procedures.
Single window	Members are encouraged to establish a single window to allow traders to submit documents and data requirements.
Pre-shipment inspection	Members shall not require the use of pre-shipment inspections in relation to tariff classification and customs valuation.
Use of customs brokers	Members shall not introduce a requirement for the mandatory use of customs brokers.
Common border procedures	Members must apply the common procedures and documents for the release and clearance of goods throughout their territory.
Rejected goods	Members must allow an importer to re-consign or return the rejected goods to the exporter when the goods do not comply with SPS standards or technical regulations.
Temporary admission of goods and inward and outward processing	Members must set customs procedures for the temporary admission, inward processing, and outward processing of goods.
Transit	Members must facilitate the free transit of goods.
Customs cooperation	Members are encouraged to share information and cooperate on best practices in managing customs.

Source: Compiled from WTO, 2023a.

The Trade Cost Index of WTO[55] estimates bilateral trade costs for various economies and sectors between 2000 and 2018. The determinants of this index consist of information and transaction cost, ICT connectiveness, governance quality, transport and travel cost, trade policy and regulatory differences, and other related variables. According to that index, in the agricultural sector, transport costs account for around 25% of the total cost, followed by information and transaction costs. The costs to export declined over time for both small- and medium-sized enterprises (SMEs) and large firms; however, there is a huge disparity between the two categories, such that SMEs have higher trade costs. Gender differences are also important in trade costs. The data indicate that while export costs are higher for men than for women in certain economies, women face higher export costs in the majority of the economies examined.

Developing countries' commitments and achievements vary, and there are certain factors that affect their trade performances. Recent studies[56] show that trade facilitation commitments depend on the countries' level of development, population size, ability to deal with bureaucratic problems, and foreign aid received to support trade facilitation. Trade costs are important impediments to food trade and are related to the income levels of countries such that low-income countries are subject to high trade costs. In addition, these costs are high in agricultural trade. Initiatives such as regional trade agreements and improving transport connectivity are crucial ways of reducing trade costs. Since the relative effectiveness of these policies differs according to the country's income groups, policies can be designed taking into consideration these differences.[57]

10   Value Chains and Food Trade

In general terms, the value chain refers to the life cycle of a product or service, including material sourcing, production, consumption, reprocessing, and review stages. There are many sub-concepts regarding the concept of value chains, such as the food value chain, sustainable value chain, and global value chain (GVC). A food value chain consists of all the stakeholders who participate in the coordinated production and value-adding activities in the production of food products. In contrast, a sustainable food value chain includes efficiency (economic sustainability), social benefits (social sustainability), and improvement of environmental quality (environmental sustainability).[58] GVC refers to international production sharing in which various activities are shared by various countries. The GVC can boost developing countries' competitiveness and access to high technology.[59] Certain factors determine GVC participation. For instance, factor endowments, geography, political stability, liberal trade policies, FDI, and domestic industrial capacity are the main drivers in determining GVC participation, and these factors matter more for GVC trade than for traditional trade.[60]

The impact of GVCs on the agricultural sector varies. For instance, some producers who sell to differentiated markets can capture a larger portion of the value added and face lower volatility than mainstream producers. This process, at the same time, leads to a change in the area planted.[61] Global private regulations can lead to structural changes in trader-farmer relationships and may increase transaction costs, farm-gate prices,[62] and trade costs.[63] The GVC participation may positively affect some agricultural indicators, such as value added per worker, but upstream positioning is negatively related to the agricultural value added.[64] The benefit of the GVCs can be ensured by coordinating the private-public partnership, monitoring, and stakeholder participation. The GVCs affect trade policies as well. Recent studies[65] indicate that if domestic content in foreign final goods is high, countries have a reduced incentive to manipulate their terms of trade, leading to lower import tariffs. Therefore, GVCs have the ability to change the optimal tariff policies. GVCs role in trade policy through lobbying is possible in the food trade, especially in developing countries with food processing and trading sectors.

11   Aid for Trade and Agriculture

Trade can play a significant role in development. However, there are certain constraints, such as infrastructure and supply side capacity, faced by developing countries. The Aid for Trade (AFT) initiative was initialized at the 2005 Hong Kong WTO Ministerial Conference and aimed to mobilize resources to address the trade-related constraints faced by developing countries.[66] The OECD and WTO have established a monitoring framework in order to track the initiative that consists of mainstreaming trade, trade-related projects, enhanced capacity, and increased trade capacity to reduce poverty.[67] The initiative helps developing countries through development assistance and low concessional loans through donors. Based on the evaluations, this support helped developing countries improve their competitiveness, expand and diversify their trade, attract foreign investment, and empower women's employment.

Trade diversification can improve competitiveness and reduce certain volatilities in global markets. Trade diversification includes product diversification, geographical diversification, and historical performance. The diversification index indicates to what extent the structure of exports or imports by product of a given economy or region differs from the world pattern.[68] Diversification index ranges from 0 to 1, and the index value closer to 1 indicates a bigger difference from the world average. Table 11.1 presents the export diversification index by region. The data indicate that Northern America and Western Europe have high levels of export diversification, while Northern Africa and Southern Asia have the lowest diversification levels. Among the regions, Sub-Saharan Africa and Oceania have made no sustainable progress over the years.

Table 11.1 Export Diversification Index by Country

| | Export Diversification Index | | |
Region	2000	2010	2022
Northern Africa	0.71	0.65	0.56
Sub-Saharan Africa	0.59	0.57	0.59
Northern America	0.20	0.21	0.20
Latin America and the Caribbean	0.30	0.35	0.38
Central Asia	0.77	0.69	0.65
Southern Asia	0.60	0.47	0.44
Eastern Europe	0.35	0.29	0.27
Western Europe	0.22	0.25	0.24
Oceania	0.52	0.61	0.71

Source: UNCTAD, 2023.

Dependence on the export of primary commodities harms developing countries, especially when prices are volatile, reducing export earnings and leading macroeconomic instabilities. That commodity dependence, especially in primary commodities, raises vulnerability because of the declining trend of non-oil primary commodity prices in the long term.[69] In improving export diversification, institutions, human capital, and GDP per capita play significant roles for developing countries.[70] On the other hand, export quality emerges as an important variable in global markets. The export of high-quality food products raises export incomes and improves the welfare of the producers, especially in developing countries. The export quality index is based on unit values, and higher values for the quality indices indicate a higher quality level. IMF database on the export quality index for the latest available year indicates that the value is high in developed countries but low in developing countries, especially in the Sub-Saharan region.[71]

As can be seen in Figure 11.1, the improvement in food quality can be achieved through research and development, good agricultural practices, food processing, extension and training, and an appropriate marketing mix.

Nation-level food safety regulations, in tandem with global regulations and guidelines, are necessary for both domestic and international consumer health and environmental quality. These regulations should be developed and implemented in liaison with related stakeholders and should include control and reinforcement mechanisms to be fully efficient. Research and development in the food industry is costly and requires government support, especially in developing countries. However, given the fact that R&D yields high value-added products in the long run, the benefits certainly outweigh the short-term costs. Good agricultural practices (GAPs) towards the products marketed in food export markets include risk assessment, product-level food safety standards, integrated pest management, conservation of natural resources, harvesting procedures, storage, transportation, traceability, environmental management, and certification systems.

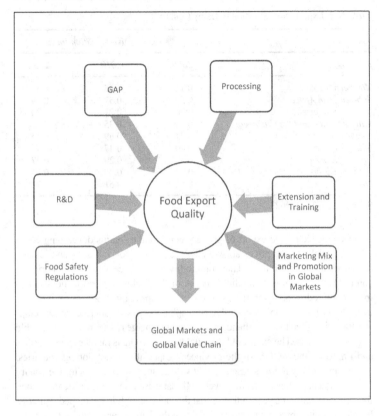

Figure 11.1 Drivers of Food Export Quality

Given the fact that processed food products have a high value compared to unprocessed ones, designing various support and incentive policies in the agricultural sector yields higher export earnings. Extension and training activities carried out in collaboration with producers' organizations, government, and research centers are quite effective in delivering the outcomes of research activities aiming for high-value production and marketing to the producers. Marketing strategies for export markets include marketing research, choosing appropriate food products for export markets based on partner country characteristics, pricing strategy, logistics, and promotion activities in global markets. Through implementing a successful food export strategy, developing countries can improve the welfare of agricultural producers and actively participate in GVCs.

Recently, endogenous growth models attempted to answer the interaction between diversification in trade and growth.[72] In the classical Solow model, capital accumulation depends on investment, technological progress is considered exogenous, and positive progress in the technology or labor force is necessary to achieve steady-state growth. In the endogenous growth models, employing trade interaction, including knowledge spillovers and continual growth of new products with differentiated intermediate inputs, leads to the continual growth of the GDP. Another implication of the endogenous growth models is the importance of the scale effect, such that higher amounts of labor in terms of effective R&D leads to higher growth rates. However, this implication is valid in the long run and somewhat ambiguous in the short run. The recent advancements in new trade theories imply a certain level of the link between the firms' export diversity, income, and average sectoral productivity. When trade-oriented firms are more productive than domestic ones, the greater share of exporters improves the income and growth of an economy. Certainly, further research is needed in that area. In terms of developing economics, there is some evidence that export diversity can serve as a crucial determinant for low-income countries.[73]

12   Gender and Food Trade

Trade's role in the empowerment of women is incontestable. Women participate in trade activities as entrepreneurs, traders, workers, and consumers. The available evidence indicates that[74] women tend to concentrate on SMEs, and these activities are not always reflected in trade data. In 2017, the WTO members agreed to a Joint Declaration on Trade and Women's Economic Empowerment, which aims to promote women's participation in trade.[75] There are some areas where trade policies play an important role in trade promotion regarding gender. Gender-differentiated impact analysis in the areas of evaluation of trade policies and trade agreements is necessary to understand the specific issues related to the trade-gender interaction. Implementing trade-facilitating reforms that reduce fees and charges and simplify the border trade procedures benefit women working in export-oriented SMEs. Lower trade barriers on essential commodities lead to lower prices and higher purchasing power in low-income countries where women's role is essential in households. The inclusiveness of gender-related preferential trade agreements (PTAs) can promote cooperation among developing countries on gender issues.[76]

Trade can expand women's economic role, decrease inequality, and improve access to education. For instance, exporters employ more women in trade-related sectors than in domestic sectors in developing countries. In addition, trade increases in women's wages help improve equality. The change in the global economy offers new opportunities for women in services, GVCs, and digital technology. However, certain challenges exist to women's participation in the labor force, and they are also overrepresented in informal trade, especially in Sub-Saharan Africa. The lack of gender-specific data causes difficulty in formulating gender-specific trade policies.[77] Since in most developing countries, agriculture and agribusiness sectors play a major role in production and trade, and promoting gender-specific trade policies in these sectors certainly improves sustainable development in these regions.

Courses in higher education, such as vocational education, and fields of studies related to agriculture, related to entrepreneurship, gender equality, and women's empowerment, can play a significant role in sustainable development, especially in developing countries. It should be underlined that a significant number of students come from rural areas, and when equipped with critical skills related to women's entrepreneurship, they can contribute to regional development activities after graduation. Some success stories exist in certain countries where these types of programs are carried out in collaboration with local governments, chambers, and commodity exchanges. In particular, it should be noted that women's participation in the labor force is necessary but insufficient for sustainable development. Quality of the working environment needs to be established, and social security rights need to be safeguarded by legal frameworks and regulations to ensure an equitable and prosperous society.

13   Voluntary Standards and Food Trade

Voluntary sustainability standards (VSS) are private standards that require products to meet specific economic, social, and environmental sustainability criteria. The requirements cover product quality, production and processing methods, and transportation. These standards are mostly designed and marketed by NGOs or private firms.[78] In terms of the impact of these standards on global trade, certification systems such as GlobalGAP are found to be positive,[79] and HACCP has a limited impact compared to mandatory standards on certain food exports.[80] The studies examining the impact of these standards on the quality found that the voluntary standards also help improve the quality of imports of food products.[81] The Fairtrade certification is found to be a significant factor in increasing the incomes of smallholder households and reducing poverty.[82]

In terms of smallholder market participation and voluntary standards, FAO[83] has certain observations and strategic recommendations. According to these observations, financial and human resource capabilities at the farm level determine compliance with the standards. Institutional support towards smallholders is necessary but insufficient in some regions. Therefore, it is necessary to form organizations in order to participate in certified value chains efficiently. The voluntary standards combined with mandatory standards can contribute to the well-being of consumers and export revenues of developing countries. Establishing an efficient standard environment requires long-term investment, and public-private partnership is certainly an important factor in achieving sustainable outcomes. As in the case of many initiatives, regular monitoring and ex-post impact assessments are required to evaluate the efficiency of the related schemes and determine certain factors that need improvement.

Notes

1 WTO, World Trade Report. Trade and public policies: A closer look at non-tariff measures in the 21st century (Geneva, 2012).

2 See FAO (2017).

3 UNCTAD, International Classification of Non-Tariff Measures (Geneva, 2019).

4 STDF, Systems *Approaches in Food Safety and Plant Health* - SPS Committee Side Event, (2022).

5 See Cadot (2018) for a detailed information.

6 Patricia Augier, et al., "The impact of rules of origin on trade flows," *Economic Policy*, 20(43), (2005):569–624.

7 See UNCTAD (2017) for detailed information on the NTMs database.

8 UNCTAD, The-Unseen Impact of Non-Tariff Measures: Insights from a New Database (2017).

9 European Commission, Food Safety (2017).

10 WTO, *Sanitary and Phytosanitary Measures*, (2022a).

11 Ibid.

12 Ibid.

13 See Atici (2013).

14 Chunlai Chen, et al., "Measuring the effect of food safety standards on China's agricultural exports," *Review of World Economics*, 144, (2018):83–106.

15 Juthathip Jongwanich, "The impact of food safety standards on processed food exports from developing countries," *Food Policy*, 34, (2009):447–457.

16 Miet Maertens, Johan F.M. Swinnen, "Trade, standards, and poverty: Evidence from Senegal," *World Development*, 37, (2008):161–178.

17 Sven M. Anders, Julie A. Caswell, "Standards as barriers versus standards as catalysts: Assessing the impact of HACCP implementation on US seafood imports," *American Journal of Agricultural Economics*, 91, (2009):310–321.

18 Steven Jaffe, Spencer Henson, "Standards and agro-food exports from developing countries: Rebalancing the debate," *World Bank Policy Research Working Paper* 3348, (2004).

19 Cemal Atici, "Food Safety Regulations and Export Responses of Developing Countries: The Case of Turkey's Fig and Hazelnut Exports," *FAO Commodity and Trade Policy Research Working Paper No: 39.* (Rome, 2013).

20 Esteban Ferro, Tsunehiro Otsuki, John S. Wilson, "The effect of product standards on agricultural exports," *Food Policy*, 50, (2015):68–79.

21 Cemal Atici, "Use of the dispute settlement mechanism of the WTO by developing Countries in the context of food safety," *Global Trade and Customs Journal*, 13(3), (2018):107–115.

22 FAO, "Biotechnologies for Agricultural Development" Proceedings of the FAO International Technical Conference on "Agricultural Biotechnologies in Developing Countries: Options and Opportunities in Crops, Forestry, Livestock, Fisheries and Agro-industry to Face the Challenges of Food Insecurity and Climate Change" (ABDC-10), (2011a).

23 Ibid.

24 Clive James, Global Status of Commercialized Biotech/GM Crops: 2013. ISAAA Brief Highlights, (2019). Highlights. No. 44. http://www.isaaa.org [Accessed September 29, 2022].

25 FAO, *Statistical Yearbook* (Rome, 2012).

26 See Atici (2014) for a detailed discussion on the issue.

27 Ibid.

28 Ibid.

29 WTO, *Technical Barriers to Trade*, (2022b).

30 Anne-Celia Disdier, et al., "The impact of regulations on agricultural trade: Evidence from the SPS and TBT agreements," American *Journal of Agricultural Economics*, 90(2), (2008):336–350.

31 Andreas C. Drichoutis, et al., "Consumer preferences for fair labour certification," *European Review of Agricultural Economics*, 44(3), (2017):455–474.

32 Nicholas DiMarcello, et al., "Global fair trade markets and product innovations," *Eurochoices*, 13(3), (2014):12–17.

33 WTO, TRIPS- Trade-Related Aspects of Intellectual Property Rights (2022c).

34 Mercedes Campi, Marco Deuenas, "Intellectual property rights and international trade of agricultural products," *World Development*, 80, (2016):1–18.

35 Zakaria Sorgho, Bruno Larue, "Geographical indication regulation and intra-trade in the European Union," *Agricultural Economics*, 45, (2014):1–12.

36 Martijn Huysmans, Johan Swinnen, "No terroir in the cold? A note on the geography of geographical indications," *Journal of Agricultural Economics*, 70(2), (2019):550–559.

37 Claude Henry, Joseph E. Stiglitz, "Intellectual property, dissemination of innovation and sustainable development," *Global Policy*, 1(3), (2010):237–251.

38 UNCTAD, *NTMs from A to Z*, (2022a).

39 FAO, World Food Summit. Rome Declaration on World Food Security, (1996a).

40 FAO, Food Security. Policy Brief. Issue 2, (1996b).

41 FAO, IFAD, UNICEF, WFP and WHO, The State of Food Security and Nutrition in the World 2022. Repurposing food and agricultural policies to make healthy diets more affordable (Rome, 2022).

42 FAO, *Food Loss and Food Waste*, (2022a).

43 Joseph W. Glauber, "Trade and climate change: The role of reforms in ensuring food security and sustainability" (IFPRI, 2022).

44 Mercedes Campi, et al., "Specialization in food production affects global food security and food systems sustainability," *World Development*, 141(105411), (2021):1–19.

45 Meidad Kissinger, "International trade related food miles- The case of Canada," *Food Policy*, 37(2), (2012):171–178.

46 Alan Matthews, "Trade rules, food security and the multilateral trade negotiations," *European Review of Agricultural Economics*, 41(3), (2014):511–535.

47 Cemal Atici, Income Distribution Impacts of the Changes in Turkey's Foreign Trade and Transfer Policies: A Social Accounting Matrix Approach. Agricultural Economics Research Institute, Publication No: 114 (Ankara, 2004).

48 Cristopher Barrett, "Immiserized growth in liberalized agriculture," *World Development*, 26(5), (1998):743–753.

49 Sinan Ciftci, Cemal Atici, "WTO reforms and their impacts on the agricultural export of the developing countries," *Turkish Journal of Agricultural Economics*, 24(1), (2018):11–120.

50 Donald Mitchell, "A Note on Rising Food Prices," *World Bank Policy Research Working Paper* 4682, (2008).

51 Bernardina Algieri, Arturo Leccadito, "Price volatility and speculative activities in futures commodity markets: A combination of combinations of p-values test," *Journal of Commodity Markets*, 13, (2019):4054.

52 FAO, *Price Volatility and Food Security*, Committee on Food Security, (2011b).

53 WTO, *Trade Facilitation*, (2022d).

54 Ibid.

55 See WTO 2023b and Peter H. Egger, et al., "Trade Cost in a Global Economy: Measurement, Aggregation, and Decomposition," WTO ESRD Staff Working Paper ERSD-2021-2 (2021).

56 Russell Hillberry, Carlos Zurita, "Commitment behaviour in the world trade organization's trade facilitation agreement," *The World Economy*, 45(1), (2022):36–75.

57 Jean-Francois Arvis, et al., "Trade costs in the developing world: 1996–2010," *World Trade Review*, 15(3), (2016):451–474.

58 FAO, *Sustainable Food Value Chains Knowledge Platform*, (2022b); David Neven, *Developing Sustainable Food Value Chains. Guiding Principles* (Rome, 2014).

59 World Bank, *Global Value Chains*, (2022b).

60 Ana Margarida Fernandes, et al., "Determinants of global value chain participation: Cross-country evidence," *The World Bank Economic Review*, 36(2), (2022):329–360.

61 Ximena Rueda, Eric F. Lambin, "Linking globalization to local land uses: How eco-consumers and gourmands are changing the Colombian coffee landscapes," *World Development*, 41, (2013):286–301.

62 Jeff Neilson, "Global private regulation and value-chain restructuring in Indonesian smallholder coffee systems," *World Development*, 36(9), (2008):1607–1622.

63 Laura M.G. Hidalgo, et al., "Multiplicity of sustainability standards and potential trade costs in the palm oil industry," *Agribusiness*, 39(1), (2023):263–284.

64 Pierluigi Montalbano, Silvia Nenci, "Does global value chain participation and positioning in the agriculture and food sectors affect economic performance? A global assessment," *Food Policy*, 108, (2022):1–12.

65 Emily J. Blanchard, et al., *Global Supply Chains and Trade Policy*. NBER Working Paper Series, 21883, (2017).

66 WTO, *Aid for Trade*, (2022e).

67 OECD, *Aid for Trade*, (2022a).

68 UNCTAD (2023).

69 See UNDP (2011).

70 Patrick N. Osakwe, et al., "Trade dependence, liberalization and exports diversification in developing countries," UNCTAD Research Paper No.2, (2019).

71 See IMF (2023).

72 For a detailed discussion on the subject see Feenstra and Kee (2008).

73 Theo S. Eicher, David J. Kuenzel, "The elusive effects of trade on growth: Export diversity and economic take-off," *Canadian Journal of Economics*, 49(1), (2016):264–295.

74 OECD, *Trade and Gender*, (2022b).

75 WTO, Joint Declaration on Trade and Women's Economic Empowerment on the Occasion of the WTO Ministerial Conference in Buenos Aires, (2022f).

76 Jane Korinek, et al., "Trade and Gender: A Framework of Analysis," *OECD Trade Policy Paper*, 246 (2021).

77 World Bank-WTO, *Women and Trade: The Role of Trade in Promoting Gender Equality* (Washington, DC, 2020).

78 UNCTAD, *Voluntary Sustainability Standards*, (2022b).

79 Anna Andersson, "The trade effect of private standards," European *Review of Agricultural Economics*, 46(2), (2019):267–290.

80 Axel Mangelsdorf, et al., "Food standards and exports: Evidence for China," *World Trade Review*, 11(3), (2012):507–526.

81 Alessandro Olper, et al., "Do food standards affect the quality of EU imports?" *Economics Letters*, 122(2), (2014):233–237.

82 Brian Chiputwa, et al., "Food standards, certification, and poverty among coffee farmers in Uganda," *World Development*, 66, (2015):400–412.

83 FAO, Impact of international voluntary standards on smallholder market participation in developing countries. A review of the literature (Rome, 2014).

References

Algieri, B., Leccadito, A. (2019). Price volatility and speculative activities in futures commodity markets: A combination of combinations of p-values test. *Journal of Commodity Markets*, 13, 4054.

Anders, S.M., Caswell, J.A. (2009). Standards as barriers versus standards as catalysts: Assessing the impact of HACCP implementation on US seafood imports. *American Journal of Agricultural Economics*, 91, 310–321.

Andersson, A. (2019). The trade effect of private standards. *European Review of Agricultural Economics*, 46(2), 267–290.

Arvis, J.F., Duval, Y., Shepherd, B., Utokham, C., Raj, A. (2016). Trade costs in the developing world: 1996–2010. *World Trade Review*, 15(3), 451–474.

Atici, C. (2004). Income distribution impacts of the changes in Turkey's foreign trade and transfer policies: A social accounting matrix approach. *Agricultural Economics Research Institute*, Publication No: 114. Ankara [*In Turkish*].

Atici, C. (2013). Food Safety Regulations and Export Responses of Developing Countries: The Case of Turkey's Fig and Hazelnut Exports. FAO Commodity and Trade Policy Research Working Paper No: 39. Rome.

Atici, C. (2014). Low levels of genetically modified crops in international food and feed trade: FAO international survey and economic analysis. FAO Commodity and Trade Policy Research Working Paper No. 44. Rome.

Atici, C. (2018). Use of the dispute settlement mechanism of the WTO by developing countries in the context of food safety. *Global Trade and Customs Journal*, 13(3), 107–115.

Augier, P., Gasiorek, M., Lai Tong, C. (2005). The impact of rules of origin on trade flows. *Economic Policy*, 20(43), 569–624.

Blanchard, E.J., Bown, C.P., Johnson, R.C. (2017). Global Supply Chains and Trade Policy. *NBER Working Paper Series*, 21883.

Barrett, C.B. (1998). Immiserized growth in liberalized agriculture. *World Development*, 26(5), 743–753.

Cadot, O., Gourdon, J., van Tongeren, F. (2018). Estimating Ad Valorem Equivalents of Non-Tariff Measures: Combining Price-Based and Quantity-Based Approaches, OECD Trade Policy Papers, No. 215, OECD Publishing, Paris.

Campi, M., Deuenas, M. (2016). Intellectual property rights and international trade of agricultural products. *World Development*, 80, 1–18.

Campi, M., Duenas, M., Fagiolo, G. (2021). Specialization in food production affects global food security and food systems sustainability. *World Development*, 141(105411), 1–19.

Chen, C., Yang, J., Findlay, C. (2008). Measuring the effect of food safety standards on China's agricultural exports. *Review of World Economics*, 144, 83–106.

Chiputwa, B., Spielman, D.J., Qaim, M. (2015). Food standards, certification, and poverty among coffee farmers in Uganda. *World Development*, 66, 400–412.

Ciftci, S., Atici, C. (2018). WTO reforms and their impacts on the agricultural export of the developing countries. *Turkish Journal of Agricultural Economics*, 24(1), 11–120.

DiMarcello III, N., Marconi, N., Hooker, N.H. (2014). Global fair trade markets and product innovations. *Eurochoices*, 13(3), 12–17.

Disdier, A.C., Fontagne, L., Mimouni, M. (2008). The impact of regulations on agricultural trade: Evidence from the SPS and TBT agreements. *American Journal of Agricultural Economics*, 90(2), 336–350.

Drichoutis, A., Vassilopoulos, A., Lusk, J., Nayga, R.M. (2017). Consumer preferences for fair labour certification. *European Review of Agricultural Economics*, 44(3), 455–474.

Egger, P.H., Larch, M., Nigai, S., Yotov, Y.V. (2021). *Trade Cost in a Global Economy: Measurement, Aggregation, and Decomposition.* WTO ESRD Staff Working Paper ERSD-2021-2.

Eicher, T.S., Kuenzel, D.J. (2016). The elusive effects of trade on growth: Export diversity and economic take-off. *Canadian Journal of Economics*, 49(1), 264–295.

European Commission, Food Safety (2017). https://ec.europa.eu/food/overview_en [Accessed September 22, 2022].

FAO (1996a). World Food Summit. Rome Declaration on World Food Security. https://www.fao.org/3/w3613e/w3613e00.htm [Accessed October 5, 2022].

FAO (1996b). *Food Security. Policy Brief.* Issue 2.

FAO (2011a). *Biotechnologies for Agricultural Development.* Proceedings of the FAO International Technical Conference on "Agricultural Biotechnologies in Developing Countries: Options and Opportunities in Crops, Forestry, Livestock, Fisheries and Agro-industry to Face the Challenges of Food Insecurity and Climate Change" (ABDC-10), http://www.fao.org/docrep/014/i2300e/i2300e00.htm [Accessed September 29, 2022].

FAO (2011b). Price Volatility and Food Security. Committee on Food Security. https://www.fao.org/3/av038e/av038e.pdf [Accessed October 5, 2022].

FAO (2012). Statistical Yearbook. Rome.

FAO (2014). Impact of international voluntary standards on smallholder market participation in developing countries. A review of the literature. Rome.

FAO (2017). Non-tariff measures in agricultural trade. Trade Policy Briefs. No:26.

FAO (2022b). Sustainable Food Value Chains Knowledge Platform. https://www.fao.org/sustainable-food-value-chains/what-is-it/en/ [Accessed October 14, 2022].

FAO (2022a). Food Loss and Waste. https://www.fao.org/nutrition/capacity-development/food-loss-and-waste/en/ [Accessed November 11, 2022].

FAO, IFAD, UNICEF, WFP and WHO (2022). The State of Food Security and Nutrition in the World 2022. Repurposing food and agricultural policies to make healthy diets more affordable. Rome, FAO. https://doi.org/10.4060/cc0639en [Accessed October 4, 2022].

Feenstra, R.C., Kee, H.L. (2008). Export variety and country productivity: Estimating the monopolistic competition model with endogenous productivity. *Journal of International Economics*, 74(2), 500–518.

Feenstra, R.C. (2016). *Advanced International Trade. Theory and Evidence.* Princeton: Princeton University Press.

Fernandes, A.M., Kee, H.L., Winkler, D. (2022). Determinants of global value chain participation: Cross-country evidence. *The World Bank Economic Review*, 36(2), 329–360.

Ferro, E., Otsuki, T., Wilson, J. (2015). The effect of product standards on agricultural exports. *Food Policy*, 50, 68–79.

Glauber, J.W. (2022). Trade and climate change: The role of reforms in ensuring food security and sustainability. In 2022 Global Food Policy Report: Climate Change and Food Systems. Chapter 3. Washington, DC: International Food Policy Research Institute (IFPRI), 28–37. https://doi.org/10.2499/9780896294257_03 [Accessed October 4, 2022].

Henry, C., Stiglitz, J.E. (2010). Intellectual property, dissemination of innovation and sustainable development. *Global Policy*, 1(3), 237–251.

Hidalgo, L.M.G., de Faria, R.N., Souza Piao, R., Wieck, C. (2023). Multiplicity of sustainability standards and potential trade costs in the palm oil industry. *Agribusiness*, 39(1), 263–284.

Hillberry, R., Zurita, C. (2022). Commitment behaviour in the world trade organization's trade facilitation agreement. *The World Economy*, 45(1), 36–75.

Huysmans, M., Swinnen, J. (2019). No terroir in the cold? A note on the geography of geographical indications. *Journal of Agricultural Economics*, 70(2), 550–559.

IMF (2023). Export Diversification and Quality. https://data.imf.org/?sk=a093df7d-e0b8-4913-80e0-a07cf90b44db [Accessed September 29, 2023].

Jaffee, S., S. Henson (2004). Standards and agro-food exports from developing countries: Rebalancing the debate. *World Bank Policy Research Working Paper* 3348.

James, C. (2019). *Global Status of Commercialized Biotech/GM Crops: 2013*. ISAAA Brief Highlights. No. 44. http://www.isaaa.org [Accessed September 29, 2022].

Jongwanich, J. (2009). The impact of food safety standards on processed food exports from developing countries. *Food Policy*, 34, 447–457.

Kissinger, M. (2012). International trade related food miles – The case of Canada. *Food Policy*, 37(2), 171–178.

Korinek, J., Moise, E., Tange, J. (2021). Trade and Gender: A Framework of Analysis. *OECD Trade Policy Paper*, 246.

Maertens, M., Swinnen, J.F.M. (2008). Trade, standards, and poverty: Evidence from Senegal. *World Development*, 37, 161–178.

Mangelsdorf, A., Portugal-Perez, A., Wilson, J. (2012). Food standards and exports: Evidence for China. *World Trade Review*, 11(3), 507–526.

Matthews, A. (2014). Trade rules, food security and the multilateral trade negotiations. *European Review of Agricultural Economics*, 41(3), 511–535.

Mitchell, D. (2008). A Note on Rising Food Prices. World Bank Policy Research Working Paper 4682.

Montalbano, P., Nenci, S. (2022). Does global value chain participation and positioning in the agriculture and food sectors affect economic performance? A global assessment. *Food Policy*, 108, 1–12.

Neilson, J. (2008). Global private regulation and value-chain restructuring in Indonesian smallholder coffee systems. *World Development*, 36(9), 1607–1622.

Neven, D. (2014). *Developing Sustainable Food Value Chains. Guiding Principles*. Rome: FAO.

OECD (2022a). Aid for Trade. https://www.oecd.org/aidfortrade/ [Accessed October 17, 2022].

OECD (2022b). Trade and Gender. https://www.oecd.org/trade/topics/trade-and-gender/ [Accessed October 18, 2022].

Olper, A., Curzi, D., Pacca, L. (2014). Do food standards affect the quality of EU imports? *Economics Letters*, 122(2), 233–237.

Osakwe, P.N., Santos-Paulino, A.U., Dogan, B. (2019). Trade dependence, liberalization, and exports diversification in developing countries," UNCTAD Research Paper No. 2.

Rueda, X., Lambin, E.F. (2013). Linking globalization to local land uses: How eco-consumers and gourmands are changing the Colombian coffee landscapes. *World Development*, 41, 286–301.

Sorgho, Z., Larue, B. (2014). Geographical indication regulation and intra-trade in the European Union. *Agricultural Economics*, 45, 1–12.

STDF (2022). Systems Approaches in Food Safety and Plant Health - SPS Committee Side Event. https://standardsfacility.org/systems-approaches-food-safety-and-plant-health-sps-committee-side-event [Accessed December 12, 2022].

UNCTAD (2017). The-Unseen Impact of Non-Tariff Measures: Insights from a New Database. https://unctad.org/system/files/official-document/ditc-tab-MC11-UNCTAD-NTMs.pdf [Accessed December 21, 2022].

UNCTAD (2019). International Classification of Non-Tariff Measures. Geneva. https://unctad.org/system/files/official-document/ditctab2019d5_en.pdf [Accessed October 7, 2022].

UNCTAD (2022a). Non-Tariff Measures. From A to Z. UNCTAD/DITC/TAB/2021/3.

UNCTAD (2022b). Voluntary Sustainability Standards. https://unctad.org/topic/trade-analysis/voluntary-sustainability-standards [Accessed October 7, 2022].

UNCTAD (2023). UNCTADSTAT. https://unctadstat.unctad.org [Accessed September 12, 2023].

UNDP (2011). *Commodity Dependence and International Commodity Prices, in Towards Human Resilience: Sustaining MDG Progress in an Age of Economic Uncertainty*. New York: UNDP.

World Bank (2022a). WITS-Non-Tariff Measures. https://wits.worldbank.org/ [Accessed December 22, 2022].

World Bank (2022b). Global Value Chains. https://www.worldbank.org/en/topic/global-value-chains [Accessed October 14, 2022].

World Bank and World Trade Organization (2020). *Women and Trade: The Role of Trade in Promoting Gender Equality*. Washington, DC: World Bank.

WTO (2012). World Trade Report. Trade and public policies: A closer look at non-tariff measures in the 21st century. Geneva.

WTO (2022a). Sanitary and phytosanitary measures. https://www.wto.org/english/tratop_e/sps_e/sps_e.htm [Accessed October 7, 2022].

WTO (2022b). Technical barriers to trade. https://www.wto.org/english/tratop_e/tbt_e/tbt_e.htm [Accessed October 7, 2022].

WTO (2022c). TRIPS- Trade-Related Aspects of Intellectual Property Rights. https://www.wto.org/english/tratop_e/trips_e/trips_e.htm [Accessed October 7, 2022].

WTO (2022d). Trade Facilitation. https://www.wto.org/english/tratop_e/tradfa_e/tradfa_e.htm [Accessed October 12, 2022].

WTO (2023b). Trade Cost Index. http://tradecosts.wto.org [Accessed September 21, 2023].

WTO (2022e). Aid for Trade. https://www.wto.org/english/tratop_e/devel_e/a4t_e/aid4trade_e.htm [Accessed October 17, 2022].

WTO (2022f). Joint Declaration on Trade and Women's Economic Empowerment on the Occasion of the WTO Ministerial Conference in Buenos Aires in December 2017. https://www.wto.org/english/thewto_e/minist_e/mc11_e/genderdeclarationmc11_e.pdf [Accessed October 18, 2022].

WTO (2023a). Trade Facilitation Agreement Database. https://www.tfadatabase.org/en/measures [Accessed September 20, 2023].

Part IV
Trade, Environment, and Agriculture

14   Food Trade and Environment Interaction

The impact of free trade on the environment varies depending on the environmental regulations and policies. In a partial equilibrium setting, when a country moves from autarky to free trade, there are several cases to consider:[1] an importing or exporting country imposing an efficient environmental tax and an importing or exporting country imposing no such taxes. Trade liberalization in commodities whose production pollutes the environment may have welfare-enhancing or -deteriorating impacts depending on the domestic environmental tax. For instance, if a country does not impose an environmental tax on production, the import benefits the country's welfare due to a decrease in resource cost and domestic pollution levels. If a country does not impose an environmental tax and becomes a net exporter of the polluting sector, the net welfare impact is unclear, depending on the relative sizes of environmental costs and trade gains. When pollution taxes are imposed, the liberalized trade benefits the country no matter if the country is an importer or exporter because trade gains outweigh the environmental damage. Taxes and subsidies on the trade of related commodities are inferior to domestic environmental policies due to their impact on prices. In the general equilibrium setting,[2] it was demonstrated that trade liberalization would benefit a small country, provided that the environmental tax is set optimally.

The levels of economic development affect environmental degradation differently. Based on the hypothesis that there exists an inverted U-shape relation between the level of income inequality,[3] the Environmental Kuznets Curve (EKC) suggests that at the beginning of economic development, quantity and intensity of environmental degradation is limited, as economic development accelerates with the intensification of agriculture and extraction of other resources the rate of resource depletion increases; however, at the higher levels of development and due to environmental awareness and regulations environmental degradation decreases.[4]

Trade-related environmental effects can be classified as scale effect, structural effect, product effect, technical effect, and regulatory effect.[5] Increasing trade flow can have positive or negative effects on the environment through

DOI: 10.4324/9781032708577-5

the change in product composition of trade (product effect), by increasing economic growth and generating the funds available for environmental protection (scale effect), by altering the location, product-mix, and intensity of production by the removal of trade distortive and environmentally harmful subsidies (structural effect), by using more efficient technologies (technical effect), and by creating greater consciousness of, and higher standards regarding, the environment because of the higher income generated by trade-related flows (regulatory effect).[6] The process of globalization may provide a comparative advantage in pollution-intensive production among countries due to differences in environmental regulations, and it is called the pollution haven hypothesis (PHH).[7] Trade openness also increases the flow of FDI and may have various impacts on environmental degradation.

Since then, numerous studies have searched the trade openness, FDI, and EKC hypothesis for various countries and sectors utilizing different methodologies. In an earlier study, stimulations found that global emissions continue to rise, forest loss stabilizes, but tropical deforestation continues in the long term.[8] In econometric studies, environmental governance, geographic vulnerability,[9] and energy use per capita[10] are found to be significant factors for emission levels. In terms of the impact of FDI on environmental degradation, FDI-PHH holds in some provinces,[11] in joint ventures,[12] and even among high-income economies,[13] while the stringency of regulations may reduce the FDI flow,[14] and in some cases, the FDI has no deteriorating effect on the environmental quality[15] at the regional level. On the other hand, environmental provisions in preferential trade agreements (PTAs) can help reduce dirty exports and increase green exports from developing countries.[16] General equilibrium studies examining the trade-environment interaction found that energy use, emission levels, and polluting input use rise in developing countries.[17] However, the emission levels can be reduced in some regions by emission trading mechanisms.[18]

Based on the findings of the studies, a few implications can be drawn in terms of trade, development, and sustainable development. Energy consumption increases in tandem with globalization, and countries need environmentally cleaner technologies in energy production to achieve sustainable development. The design of trade agreements matters, and environmental provisions can be used to promote green transformation, especially in PTAs. The stringency of regulations can help improve environmental quality and attract sustainable FDI for a greener economy. Emission trading can play an important role in environmental quality. However, based on the current implementation of the mechanism, the EU Emission Trading Scheme (ETS) has several implications for developing countries, such as legal frameworks, efficiency, capacity building, the role of agriculture, and regional collaboration to address climate change. For instance, a related study indicates that the approach for ETS allowances in member states differs,[19] which causes certain legal uncertainties. The uncertainty related to the definition leads to various interpretations, and these differences may have a deterrent effect in constructing efficient markets. Developing countries can benefit from the

EU's experiences in establishing a legal framework to design more efficient carbon pricing.[20] In addition, over-allocation of emissions and price volatility are major issues to deal with. World Bank[21] sets principles for successful pricing called FASTER (fairness, alignment of policies and objectives, stability and predictability, transparency, efficiency and cost-effectiveness, reliability, and environmental integrity).

14.1   Environmental Policy Instruments

Environmental policies include three main types of instruments: market-based incentives, command-and-control mechanisms, and government involvement in production and enforcement.[22] The market-based incentives include effluent charges, tradeable permits, input-output taxes, and subsidies. The command-and-control measures include emission regulations such as quotas. Government involvement includes expenditures for cleanup, waste disposal, enforcement, and development or incentives for cleaner technologies.[23] The classification of the environmental policy instruments is presented in Figure 14.1.

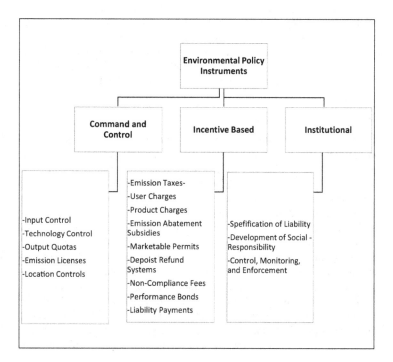

Figure 14.1 Environmental Policy Instruments

The use of various environmental instruments is a matter of environmental policy discussion. Carbon taxation policy may have various impacts on the economy and the environment. Although these types of policies reduce emission levels, one of the negative impacts of such policies is the decrease in competitiveness of the energy-intensive sectors; therefore, tax exemptions or reimbursement policies can be used in trade-oriented production activities.[24] Sometimes, the emission control targets might be costly and cause adverse employment effects in developing economies, requiring a decrease in existing conventional taxes.[25]

The major concern with tradable permits is that the cost of meeting the fixed level of emissions may be greater than initially perceived levels. In addition, volatile emission prices and uncertainties in long-term investment plans are major drawbacks. On the other hand, carbon taxes are difficult to impose globally, and hidden subsidies may offset the expected impacts. In the presence of uncertainties, taxes and subsidies produce different results. In this case, the use of hybrid control instruments[26] is recommended.

For certain, achieving economic growth in a sustainable way may require carbon taxes.[27] Since the cost of monitoring emission levels and enforcing the abatement can be high in developing countries due to technological or institutional reasons, indirect taxes or subsidies for inputs or outputs can be used as alternative policy tools.[28] Sometimes, the combination of these instruments can be used to alleviate emissions and achieve sustainable development. Considering the long-term impacts of research and development on growth and development, the optimal environmental policies can be designed to include both carbon taxes and research subsidies for cleaner technologies.[29]

14.2   Flexibility Mechanisms

The Kyoto Protocol, enforced in 2005, set three main flexibility mechanisms to deal with climate change collaboratively. These mechanisms are international emissions trading (ET), clean development mechanism (CDM), and joint implementation (JI). In addition, the parties with commitments (Annex B countries) agreed to limit or reduce emissions.[30] On the other hand, the Paris Agreement introduced the Sustainable Development Mechanism. Based on Article 6 of the Agreement, the parties were permitted to use international emissions trading, and new market and non-market mechanisms were intended to be supported.[31] The Paris Agreement introduced nationally determined contributions (NDCs) that enable each member country to reduce national emissions and employ adaptation and mitigation strategies for climate change.[32]

There are certain types of issues related to the implementation of emission trading. The EU report[33] indicates that the approach for ETS allowances in member states differs, and that situation causes certain legal uncertainties. According to the report, Directive 2003/87/EC does not specify the legal nature of the traded allowances. The uncertainty surrounding the definition leads to various interpretations. For instance, allowances are classified as a property, a right, or a financial instrument in the member states' legislation. Therefore, the differences in these definitions may have a deterrent effect in constructing efficient markets. Surely, developing countries can benefit from the EU's experiences in setting out a legal framework to design carbon pricing policies and related measures.[34]

In achieving sustainable climate goals, carbon pricing is essential and incorporates various elements such as capital flow, mobilizing knowledge, and reducing emissions. Mainly, there are two mechanisms available for carbon pricing: emissions trading and carbon tax. A World Bank report[35] estimates that 57 carbon pricing initiatives are implemented globally; however, the amount of carbon emissions covered by carbon pricing and price levels are not enough to meet the objectives of the Paris Agreement. The report indicates that global initiatives cover only 20% of greenhouse emissions, and only 5% have price levels in line with the estimates for achieving the goals of the related Agreement. In that context, international collaboration towards interregional ETS, linking national markets for greater depth and liquidity, implicit carbon price policies such as carbon tax and the elimination of fossil fuel subsidies, and private sector involvement through using carbon pricing in financial decisions are crucial to achieving a successful ETS.[36]

The efficiency of the ETS and related issues have been examined in a few studies. A study[37] testing the theory of emissions trading based on experiments in the six largest industrial regions in the EU implies that both auctions and bilateral sequential trading converge to market equilibrium. However, not all countries benefit from trade due to imperfect market structures. Another related study measuring the efficiency of the EU ETS employing the efficient market hypothesis (EMH) finds that although the trial and learning period (Phase I) was inefficient, the next period (Phase II) implied the restoration of market efficiency.[38]

The CDM is a market-based approach and aims to reduce emissions through investments in developing countries. The mechanism enables Annex B countries to invest in emission-reduction projects in developing countries. In these projects, certified emission reduction (CER) credits are issued, and developed countries can buy CERs and use them to achieve their emission reduction targets under the Kyoto Protocol.[39] The main criticisms of the CDM mechanism are related to access to formal international institutions and foreign aid[40] and failure to reduce poverty.[41] Strong industrial and energy policy in a host country[42] plays a crucial role in the development of the CDM. The EU's rule for special import quotas for CERs from the least developed countries may not be enough[43] if the barriers to project implementation are not overcome. These critiques should be taken into consideration for improvements in the related mechanisms.[44]

The UNEP database[45] related to the CDM projects indicates that most of the beneficiary host countries are in the category of middle-income countries (94%), while low-income countries account for only 2% of the CDM projects hosted, although they represent around 15% of the total countries. Based on the outcomes of these data, the findings show that low-income countries could not efficiently benefit from the CDM projects due to a lack of technical capacity to access the mechanism. In addition, the database reveals that almost 70% of the projects are hosted by China and India alone.[46]

Joint implementation (JI) is the mechanism defined in Article 6 of the Kyoto Protocol. This mechanism enables a country with an emissions reduction or limitation commitment (Annex B Party) to earn emissions reduction units (ERUs) from an emissions reduction or emissions removal project in another Annex B Party. This mechanism provides related parties with a flexible and cost-efficient means of fulfilling commitments. On the other hand, the host party benefits from this mechanism through foreign investment and technology transfer. This mechanism involves two procedures, Track 1 and Track 2. When a host party meets all the eligibility requirements to transfer and acquire ERUs, it may issue the appropriate quantity of ERUs upon verification. This procedure is referred to as the Track 1 procedure. When a host party does not meet all eligibility requirements, the verification of emission reductions needs to be implemented through the verification procedure under the Joint Implementation Supervisory Committee (JISC). This procedure is called the Track 2 procedure, and an independent entity accredited by the JISC determines whether the relevant requirements were met in order for the host party to issue and transfer ERUs.[47] According to the UNEP database on the JI mechanism,[48] most of the JI projects are CH4 reduction projects covering (gas pipeline leaks) (40%) and energy efficiency improvements (29%).

The ETS is more relevant for the agricultural sector among these three mechanisms. Agriculture accounts for a high share of GDP in many developing countries,[49] and agriculture and related land use account for 17% of total greenhouse gas emissions.[50] Emissions of methane (livestock activities), nitrous oxide (fertilizers and waste), and carbon dioxide (tillage, deforestation) are the main sources of greenhouse gas emissions in agriculture. Although global agricultural emissions exhibited a slight downward trend since 2000, the emissions due to agriculture displayed an upward trend in some developing countries (Africa and Asia).[51] The inclusion of agriculture in ETS is another matter of discussion. For instance, transaction costs might be high, and implementation will not be socially beneficial.[52] Thus, voluntary participation instead of mandatory participation is needed.

The inclusion of the agricultural sector will be the subject of discussion for future climate change agendas, given the fact that developing countries face certain problems, such as insufficient capacity for technical infrastructure, related inventory, and the organization of the financial markets. These issues should be addressed in line with the flexibility mechanisms of climate agreements through technical assistance and capacity building. The transition from the Kyoto Protocol to the Paris Agreement requires a certain level of preparation and commitment. In order to construct efficient ETS markets, a legal framework must be established in which the structure of the allowances and financial instruments are clearly defined. Then, efficient markets should be constructed through international and interregional collaboration. In addition, creating national and regional emissions trading schemes in line with the World Trade Organization in future negotiations is important at this stage.[53]

The implementation of CDM underlines that low-income developing countries have difficulty accessing and fully benefitting from the mechanism. Specific policy measures designed for low-income host countries, such as technical aid for accessing and implementing related projects, can encourage related parties to invest in cleaner technologies in developing countries. The JI project data reveal that most of the related projects fall into the category of the area of energy efficiency. Thus, designing infrastructure development strategies and determining the priority areas for improvement in host countries are essential for efficient implementation. Given the fact that agriculture plays a major role in the economies of low-income and middle-income developing countries, the inclusion of the agricultural sector in flexibility mechanisms, such as ETS, might be on the agenda in the middle run. However, certain issues such as high transaction costs and immature financial markets need to be addressed. The issues arising from the structural problems of developing countries should be dealt with in tandem with the flexibility mechanisms of climate agreements, such as technical assistance and capacity building.[54] There are certain tradeoffs among the SDGs. For instance, achieving no poverty goal may harm the environment.[55] In that context, in achieving the SDGs, prioritizing a different set of targets[56] and adequate performance measurements[57] are essential.

Notes

1 Kym Anderson, "The Standard Welfare Economics of Policies Affecting Trade and the Environment," in K. Anderson, R. Blackhurst, eds, *The Greening of World Trade Issues*, (London: Harvester Wheatsheaf, 1992); R. Perman, et al., *Natural Resource and Environmental Economics* (New York: Addison Wesley, 2011).
2 Brian R. Copeland, M. Scott Taylor, *Trade and the Environment. Theory and Evidence* (Princeton: Princeton University Press, 2003).
3 Simon Kuznets, "Economic growth and income inequality," *American Economic Review*, 45(1), (1955):1–28.
4 Theodore Panayotou, "Empirical Tests and Policy Analysis of Environmental Degradation at Different Stages of Economic Development," *Working Paper WP238*, (Geneva: International Labor Office, 1993).
5 OECD, *The Environmental Effects of Trade* (Paris, 1994).
6 Cemal Atici, "Carbon emissions in Central and Eastern Europe: Environmental Kuznets curve and implications for sustainable development," *Sustainable Development*, 17(3), (2009):155–160.

7 Matthew A. Cole, "Trade, the pollution haven hypothesis and the environmental Kuznets curve: Examining the linkages," *Ecological Economics*, 48(1), (2004):71–81.

8 David I. Stern, et al., "Economic growth and environmental degradation. The environmental Kuznets curve and sustainable development," *World Development*, 24(7), (1996):1151–1160.

9 Susmita Dasgupta, et al., "Environment during growth: Accounting for governance and vulnerability," *World Development*, 34(9), (2006):1597–1611.

10 Cemal Atici, "Carbon Emissions in Central and Eastern Europe," 155–160.

11 Xiaoping He, Xin. Yao, "Foreign direct investments and the environmental Kuznets Curve: New evidence from Chinese Provinces," *Emerging Markets Finance and Trade*, 53(1), (2017):12–25.

12 Judith M. Dean, et al., "Are foreign investors attracted to weak environmental regulations? Evaluating the evidence from China," *Journal of Development Economics*, 90(1), (2009):1–13.

13 Antonio Cardoso Marques, Rafaela Vital Caetano, "Do greater amounts of FDI cause higher pollution levels? Evidence from OECD countries," *Journal of Policy Modeling*, 44(1), (2022):147–162.

14 Robert J.R. Elliott, Kenichi Shimamoto, "Are ASEAN Countries Havens for Japanese Pollution-Intensive Industry?" *The World Economy*, 31(2), (2008):236–254.

15 Cemal Atici, "Carbon emissions, trade liberalization, and the Japan-ASEAN interaction: A group-wise examination," *Journal of the Japanese and International Economies*, 26(1), (2012):167–178.

16 Clara Brandi, et al., "Do environmental provisions in trade agreements make exports from developing countries greener?" *World Development*, 129, (2020):104899, 1–22.

17 Donna J. Lee, Jian Zhang, "Efficiency, equity, and environmental implications of trade liberalization: A computable general equilibrium analysis," *The Journal of International Trade & Economic Development*, 18(3), (2009):347–371.

18 Xili Ma, et al., "The role of emissions trading mechanisms and technological progress in achieving China's regional clean air target: A CGE analysis," *Applied Economics*, 51(2), (2019):155–169.

19 EC, Legal nature of EU ETS allowances. Final report. EU Publication Office (2019).

20 Cemal Atici, "Reconciling the flexibility mechanisms of climate policies towards the inclusiveness of developing countries: Commitments and prospects," *Environment Development and Sustainability*, 24, (2022):9048–9067.

21 World Bank, *State and Trends of Carbon Pricing*, (2019a).

22 Gunnar S. Eskeland, Emanuel Jimenez, "Policy instruments for pollution control in developing countries," *The World Bank Research Observer*, 7(2), (1992):145–169.

23 For a detailed information on the issue see OECD (2003).

24 Qiao-Mei Liang, et al., "Carbon taxation policy in China: How to protect energy- and trade-intensive sectors?" *Journal of Policy Modeling*, 29(2), (2007):311–333.

25 Cagatay Telli, et al., "Economics of environmental policy in Turkey: A general equilibrium investigation of the economic evaluation of sectoral emission reduction policies for climate change," *Journal of Policy Modeling*, 30(2), (2008):321–340.

26 Anthony D. Owen, "Economics Instruments for Pollution Abatement: Tradable Permits Versus Carbon Taxes," in A.A. Dorsman, J.L. Simpson, W.Westerman, eds, *Energy Economics and Financial Markets*, (Heidelberg: Springer, 2013).

27 William D. Nordhaus, "Climate and economic development. Climates past and climate change future," *World Bank Economic Review*, 7(1), (1993):355–376.

28 Gunnar S. Eskeland, Emanuel Jimenez, "Policy Instruments" (1992):145–169.

29 Daron Acemoglu, et al., "The environment and directed technical change," *The American Economic Review*, 102(1), (2012):131–166.
30 UNFCC, *The Kyoto Protocol*, (2022a).
31 UNFCC, *Paris Agreement*, (2022b).
32 For a detailed discussion of the flexibility mechanisms see Atici (2022).
33 EC, *Legal nature of EU ETS allowances. Final report*, (EU Publication Office, 2019).
34 Cemal Atici, "Reconciling the flexibility mechanisms of climate policies towards the inclusiveness of developing countries: Commitments and prospects," *Environment Development and Sustainability*, 24, (2022):9048–9067.
35 World Bank, *State and Trends of Carbon Pricing*, (2019a).
36 Cemal Atici, "Reconciling the flexibility mechanisms of climate policies" (2022):9048–9067.
37 Ger Klaassen, et al., "Testing the theory of emissions trading, experimental evidence on alternative mechanisms for global carbon trading," *Ecological Economics*, 53(1), (2005):47–58.
38 Alberto Montagloni, Frans P. de Vries, "Carbon trading thickness and market efficiency," *Energy Economics*, 32(6), (2012):1331–1336.
39 UNFCC, *Mechanisms*, (2022c).
40 Liliana B. Andonova, Yixian Sun, "Private governance in developing countries, drivers of voluntary carbon offset programs," *Global Environmental Politics*, 19(1), (2019):99–122.
41 Jo Dirix, et al., "Is the clean development mechanism delivering benefits to the poorest communities in the developing world? A critical evaluation and proposals for reform," *Environment, Development and Sustainability*, 18(3), (2016):839–855.
42 John Fay, et al., "A comparative policy analysis of the clean development mechanism in South Africa and China," *Climate and Development*, 4(1), (2011):40–53.
43 Paula Castro, A. Michaelowa, "Would preferential access measures be sufficient to overcome current barriers to CDM projects in least developed countries?" *Climate and Development*, 3(2), (2011):123–142.
44 Cemal Atici, "Reconciling the flexibility mechanisms of climate policies," 9048–9067.
45 Fenhann, *UNEP-DTU Database*, (2019).
46 Cemal Atici, "Reconciling the flexibility mechanisms of climate policies," (2022):9048–9067.
47 UNFCC, 2022c.
48 Fenhann, *UNEP-DTU Database*, (2019).
49 World Bank, *World Development Indicators*, (2019b).
50 IEA, *The Breakthrough Agenda Report*, (2022).
51 FAO, *Emissions due to Agriculture. Global, Regional, and Country Trends 2000–2018*, (2021).
52 Tiho Ancev, "Policy considerations for mandating agriculture in a greenhouse gas emissions trading scheme," *Applied Economic Perspectives and Policy*, 33(1), (2011):99–115.
53 Cemal Atici, "Reconciling the flexibility mechanisms of climate policies," 9048–9067.
54 Ibid.
55 Edward B. Barbier, Joanne.C. Burgess "Sustainable development goal indicators: Analyzing trade-offs and complementarities," *World Development*, 122, (2019):295–305; Judith M. Ament, et al., "An empirical analysis of synergies and tradeoffs between sustainable development goals," *Sustainability*, 12(8424), (2020):1–12.

56 Cemal Atici, "Reconciling the flexibility mechanisms of climate policies," 9048–9067.
57 Luis M. Fonseca, et al., "Mapping the sustainable development goals relationships," *Sustainability*, 12(3359), (2020):1–15.

References

Acemoglu, D., Aghion, P., Bursztyn, L., Hemous, D. (2012). The environment and directed technical change. *The American Economic Review*, 102(1), 131–166.

Ament, J.M., Freeman, R., Carbone, C., Vassall, A., Watts, C. (2020). An empirical analysis of synergies and tradeoffs between sustainable development goals. *Sustainability*, 12(8424), 1–12.

Ancev, T. (2011). Policy considerations for mandating agriculture in a greenhouse gas emissions trading scheme. *Applied Economic Perspectives and Policy*, 33(1), 99–115.

Anderson, K. (1992). The Standard Welfare Economics of Policies Affecting Trade and the Environment, in K. Anderson, R. Blackhurst, eds, *The Greening of World Trade Issues*. London: Harvester Wheatsheaf.

Andonova, L.B., Sun, Y. (2019). Private governance in developing countries, Drivers of voluntary carbon offset programs. *Global Environmental Politics*, 19(1), 99–122.

Atici, C. (2009). Carbon emissions in Central and Eastern Europe: Environmental Kuznets curve and implications for sustainable development. *Sustainable Development*, 17(3), 155–160.

Atici, C. (2012). Carbon emissions, trade liberalization, and the Japan-ASEAN interaction: A group-wise examination. *Journal of the Japanese and International Economies*, 26(1), 167–178.

Atici, C. (2022). Reconciling the flexibility mechanisms of climate policies towards the inclusiveness of developing countries: Commitments and prospects. *Environment Development and Sustainability*, 24, 9048–9067.

Barbier, E.B., Burgess, J.C. (2019). Sustainable development goal indicators: Analyzing trade-offs and complementarities. *World Development*, 122, 295–305.

Brandi, C., Schwab, C., Berger, A., Morin, J.F. (2020). Do environmental provisions in trade agreements make exports from developing countries greener? *World Development*, 129, 1–22.

Castro, P., Michaelowa, A. (2011). Would preferential access measures be sufficient to overcome current barriers to CDM projects in least developed countries? *Climate and Development*, 3(2), 123–142.

Cole, M.A. (2004). Trade, the pollution haven hypothesis and the environmental Kuznets curve: Examining the linkages. *Ecological Economics*, 48 (1), 71–81.

Copeland, B.R., Taylor, M.S. (2003). *Trade and the Environment. Theory and Evidence*. Princeton: Princeton University Press.

Dasgupta, S., Hamilton, K., Pandey, K., Wheeler, D. (2006). Environment during growth: Accounting for governance and vulnerability. *World Development*, 34(9), 1597–1611.

Dean, J.M., Lovely, M.E., Wang, H. (2009). Are foreign investors attracted to weak environmental regulations? Evaluating the evidence from China. *Journal of Development Economics*, 90(1), 1–13.

Dirix, J., Peeters, W., Sterckx, S. (2016). Is the clean development mechanism delivering benefits to the poorest communities in the developing world? A critical evaluation and proposals for reform. *Environment, Development and Sustainability*, 18(3), 839–855.

EC (2019). Legal nature of EU ETS allowances. Final report. Brussels: EU Publication Office.

Elliott, R.J.R., Shimamoto, K. (2008). Are ASEAN countries havens for Japanese pollution-intensive industry? *The World Economy*, 31(2), 236–254.

Eskeland, G.S., Jimenez, E. (1992). Policy instruments for pollution control in developing countries. *The World Bank Research Observer*, 7(2), 145–169.

FAO (2021). Emissions due to Agriculture. Global, regional, and country trends 2000–2018. FAOSTAT Analytical Brief 18. https://www.fao.org/3/cb3808en/cb3808en.pdf [Accessed October 12, 2023]

Fay, J., Kapfudzaruwa, F., Na, L., Matheson, J. (2011). A comparative policy analysis of the Clean Development Mechanism in South Africa and China. *Climate and Development*, 4(1), 40–53.

Fenhann, J. (2019). UNEP-DTU Database. http://www.cdmpipeline.org [Accessed October 26, 2022].

Fonseca, L.M., Domingues, J.P., Dima, A.M. (2020). Mapping the sustainable development goals relationships. *Sustainability*, 12(3359), 1–15.

He, X., Yao, X. (2017). Foreign direct investments and the environmental Kuznets Curve: New evidence from Chinese Provinces. *Emerging Markets Finance and Trade*, 53(1), 12–25.

IEA (2022). The Breakthrough Agenda Report 2022. https://www.iea.org/reports/breakthrough-agenda-report-2022/ [Accessed September 24, 2023].

Klaassen, G., Nentjes, A., Smith, M. (2005). Testing the theory of emissions trading, experimental evidence on alternative mechanisms for global carbon trading. *Ecological Economics*, 53(1), 47–58.

Kuznets, S. (1955). Economic growth and income inequality. *American Economic Review*, 45(1), 1–28.

Lee, D.J., Zhang, J. (2009). Efficiency, equity, and environmental implications of trade liberalization: A computable general equilibrium analysis. *The Journal of International Trade & Economic Development*, 18(3), 347–371.

Liang, Q.M., Fan, Y., Wei, Y.M. (2007). Carbon taxation policy in China: How to protect energy- and trade-intensive sectors? *Journal of Policy Modeling*, 29(2), 311–333.

Ma, X., Wang, H., Wei, W. (2019). The role of emissions trading mechanisms and technological progress in achieving China's regional clean air target: A CGE analysis. *Applied Economics*, 51(2), 155–169.

Marques, A.C., Caetano, R.V. (2022). Do greater amounts of FDI cause higher pollution levels? Evidence from OECD countries. *Journal of Policy Modeling*, 44(1), 147–162.

Montagloni, A., de Vries, F.P. (2012). Carbon trading thickness and market efficiency. *Energy Economics*, 32(6), (2012), 1331–1336.

Nordhaus, W.D. (1993). Climate and economic development. Climates past and climate change future. *World Bank Economic Review*, 7(1), 355–376.

OECD (1994). *The Environmental Effects of Trade*. Paris.

OECD (2003). The Use of Economic Instruments for Pollution Control and Natural Resource Management in EECCA. CCNM/ENV/EAP (2003)5.

Owen, A.D. (2013). Economics Instruments for Pollution Abatement: Tradable Permits Versus Carbon Taxes, in A.A. Dorsman, J.L. Simpson, W. Westerman, eds, *Energy Economics and Financial Markets*. Heidelberg: Springer.

Panayotou, T. (1993). Empirical Tests and Policy Analysis of Environmental Degradation at Different Stages of Economic Development, Working Paper WP238 Technology and Employment Programme, Geneva: International Labor Office.

Perman, R., Ma, Y., Common, M., Maddison, D., McGilvray, J. (2011). *Natural Resource and Environmental Economics*. New York: Addison Wesley.

Stern, D.I., Common, M.S., Barbier, E.B. (1996). Economic growth and environmental degradation: The environmental Kuznets curve and sustainable development. *World Development*, 24(7), 1151–1160.

Telli, C., Voyvoda, E., Yeldan, E. (2008). Economics of environmental policy in Turkey: A general equilibrium investigation of the economic evaluation of sectoral emission reduction policies for climate change. *Journal of Policy Modeling*, 30(2), 321–340.

UNFCC (2022a). The Kyoto Protocol. https://unfccc.int/kyoto_protocol [Accessed October 26, 2022].

UNFCC (2022b). Paris Agreement. https://unfccc.int/process-and-meetings/the-paris-agreement/the-paris-agreement [Accessed October 26, 2022].

UNFCC (2022c). Mechanisms. https://unfccc.int/process/the-kyoto-protocol/mechanisms [Accessed October 26, 2022].

World Bank (2019a). State and trends of carbon pricing 2019. https://openknowledge.worldbank.org/handle/10986/31755 [Accessed October 20, 2022].

World Bank (2019b). World Development Indicators. https://data.worldbank.org/indicator/ [Accessed October 26, 2022].

Part V

Multilateral Trading System and Agriculture

15 WTO, Agriculture, and Sustainable Development

WTO, as a global organization, deals with the rules and regulations of trade aiming at trade facilitation. Trade negotiations have taken place as rounds since 1948 under the auspices of its predecessor, the General Agreement on Tariffs and Trade (GATT), from the early Annecy Round in 1949 to the Uruguay Round in 1995. The sectors covered included new areas such as agriculture, services, intellectual property rights, trade capacity, and development agenda over time.[1] The Agreement on Agriculture (AoA) entered into force in 1995 with the establishment of the organization and has three pillars: market access, domestic support, and export subsidies.[2]

Market access: In order to assure more transparent, predictable, and competitive global markets, this pillar transformed NTMS to bound tariffs and tariff reduction commitments. The tariffication package replaced agriculture-specific NTMs. Developed country members have agreed to reduce their tariffs by 36% on average and at least 15% for a single commodity over a six-year period, while developing countries have agreed to reduce the tariffs by 24% on average and with a minimum cut of 10% for a single commodity over ten years. Under the tariffication rule, the members were required to replace quantitative restrictions on imports with their estimated tariff equivalents. Although Article 4.2 of the Agreement prohibits the use of agricultural NTMs, certain exceptions[3] apply, including balance of payment provisions (Article XII, XVIII), general safeguard provisions (Article XIX), and other general exceptions (Article XX).

Domestic Support: This pillar aimed at enabling governments to design support policies with more flexibility in line with the WTO regulations. In that context, Green Box measures refer to supports with no or minimal trade-distorting impact, Amber Box measures refer to trade-distorting support measures which are subject to reduction commitments, and Blue Box measures refer to permitted support measures linked to production limitation programmes. Green box measures include government service programmes, direct payments, and development payments. All domestic support measures

DOI: 10.4324/9781032708577-6

not classified as Green and Blue Box in that context are considered as Amber Box measures.

Export Subsidies: The AoA set limitations on the use of agricultural export subsidies, such as export subsidies subject to product-specific reduction commitments and export subsidies consistent with the special and differential treatment provisions for developing countries. Developed country members are required to reduce the volume of subsidized exports by 21% over six years, while for developing countries, the corresponding reductions are 14% over ten years. In addition, developing countries may opt for special and differential treatment provisions of the Agreement for specific cases, such as marketing cost subsidies and internal transport subsidies, provided that these measures are in line with their commitments. The LDCs were excluded from the reduction commitments. In 2015, at the tenth Ministerial Conference, members agreed to abolish agricultural export subsidies. LDCs and net food-importing developing countries were granted the utilization of certain export subsidies as specified in Article 9.4 of the Agreement by the end of 2030.[4]

The Doha Development Agenda (DDA),[5] launched in 2001, aimed at prioritizing development issues such as rural development, food security, review of SPS measures, technical assistance, technology transfer for LDCs, review of special and differential trade provisions, and trade-environment interactions. The process has achieved some important agreements, such as eliminating agricultural export subsidies in 2015 and the Trade Facilitation Agreement in 2017. Indeed, the agenda faces some challenges, such as consensus on trade-environment tradeoffs, efforts and commitments towards developing countries' access to global markets, and reforming agricultural supports. The DDA's capacity-building programmes contributed to the beneficiaries in active participation in the negotiations, defining strategies, and defending interests; however, human and institutional capacity remain challenges.[6]

The UN organizations can play an important role in WTO's development agenda indirectly through its member organizations' contributions on specific issues such as food security, public stockholding, and other development-related issues.[7] In that context, related UN organizations' contribution through research, training, liaising with related international organizations, and creating a forum for related development issues certainly help capacity development and technical assistance for developing countries. WTO's DDA and agriculture-related sustainable development interaction is presented in Table 15.1. Some of the issues (SPS, Trade Facilitation, TRIPS) are already discussed in the related chapters.

Environmental Goods Agreement (EGA) of the WTO, launched in 2014, aims to eliminate tariffs on selected environment-related products, such as generating clean and renewable energy, improving energy and resource efficiency, controlling air pollution, managing waste, treating wastewater, monitoring the quality of the environment, and reducing noise pollution. This *ble 15.1* WTO's Doha Development Agenda, Sustainable Development, and Agriculture

licy Instrument	*Achievement*	*Challenges*
port Subsidies	-Elimination of agricultural export subsidies in 2015, Nairobi. -Extending the transition period for certain developing countries.	
S	-Transition period for developing countries to comply with other countries' new SPS measures. -Review of the SPS Agreement.	-Lack of developing countries' participation in setting international SPS measures. -Strict regulations that impede trade for some developing countries.
de Facilitation	Bali Package, Trade Facilitation Agreement in 2013.	Trade costs and insufficient capacity to implement for some developing countries.
IPS	-Common attitude and commitments for technology transfer to least-developed countries. -Transition period for LDCs.	-In some cases, they can be used as a protectionist instrument. -Insufficient implementation in technology transfer.
de & Environment	-Collaboration and information change between WTO and Multilateral Environmental Agreement Secretariats. - Negotiation willingness for trade barriers on environmental goods and services [i.e., catalytic converters, air filters or consultancy services on wastewater management]. -Environmental Goods Agreement (EGA). -Commitments to improve WTO rules on fishery subsidies to prevent environmental pollution. -Trade and Environment Committee's monitoring of the impact of trade policies on the environment, the intellectual property agreement and biodiversity, and labeling for environmental purposes.	-Lack of participation from developing countries, and slow progress at EGA due to different approaches on the list of goods covered. -Exclusion of NTMs at EGA. -Insufficient agri-environmental technology in the Environmental Goods (EG) list.
velopment nd Technical Assistance	-Examining problems and making recommendations on trade-related measures for small economies. -Developed countries' commitments to duty-free, quota-free market access for LDCs' products and considerations of additional measures to improve market access for these exports. -Establishing a working group on trade, debt, and finance. -Technical assistance for LDCs. -Establishment of the Doha Development Agenda Global Trust Fund.	-Insufficient institutional capacity for some developing countries.

negotiation process is particularly important in producing environmentally cleaner production processes, including the agricultural sector, due to possible technology transfer to developing countries. For instance, a study examining the host country characteristics in CDM projects found that reduction of protection in environmental goods would help technology transfer towards developing countries.[8] One of the reasons that explain the lack of developing country participation is that the majority of the goods in the list are mostly industrial goods produced by developing countries; thus, broadening the EG list can facilitate developing country participation[9]. The EG list can be expanded to cover more agri-environmental technologies, such as water saving and efficient irrigation in agricultural production.

16   The Dispute Settlement Mechanism and Food Safety Issues

World Trade Organization (WTO) agreements require governments to reveal their trade policies and practices by notifying the WTO. Surveillance of these policies through the Trade Policy Review Mechanism aims to ensure transparency at the multilateral level. However, sometimes disputes arise due to variations in the implementation of the policies. The Dispute Settlement Mechanism (DSM) consists of certain stages,[10] including consultations, panel setup, final panel reports to parties, final panel reports to WTO members, and Dispute Settlement Body (DSB) adoption. In the event of an appeal, an appeal report and adoption of the report by the DSB are additional stages. In the first consultation stage, countries try to settle the dispute themselves; if no settlement is reached, the complainant asks for a panel to be appointed. The panel prepares a final report within six months. The report becomes the DSB's ruling unless it is rejected by consensus. In addition, both sides can appeal the report. The DSB monitors implementation and can grant retaliation when a country does not comply with the rules.

16.1   Case Study: Dispute Settlement Mechanism and Food Trade

A study examining the DSM related to the SPS Agreement[11] revealed several important results. The mechanism was initially used mostly by developed countries, and developing countries started utilizing it later following complaints originating from strict food safety regulations towards their export markets. According to the database, the incidents related to animal products, followed by plant products and, in some cases, biotechnology products. Meat products rank first with 13 cases (29%), followed by fruits and vegetables (around 18%). Conventional food products account for 93% of incidents, while biotech products account for 7% of all incidents. Many of the disputes between developing and developed countries relate to the measures applied for fruits and vegetables, and animal products.

In contrast, most disputes among developed countries relate to the approval and marketing of biotech products. Many of the complainants and respondents are from developed countries. According to the database, most disputes over the period are related to developed countries (70%). In addition, most of the complainants and respondents (67% and 73%, respectively) are from developed countries. The majority of disputes (53%) are between developed countries, followed by the developing country as a complainant and the developed country as a respondent (20%). The disputes between developing countries as complainants and developed countries as respondents are the lowest (13%). These data reveal that developed countries utilize the dispute settlement mechanism mostly. Regional disparity also exists in the incidents. Most of the time, the mechanism was used by Northern American WTO members (42%), followed by European WTO members.

In addition, the high-income economies account for around 30 cases (67% of the incidents) as initiators in the DSM. In contrast, lower-middle-income economies have a limited share (11%), and low-income economies have no share. Most of the time, the disputes were settled with a mutually agreed solution (38%). However, in many cases, the incidents were classified, as in the case of consultation, establishment of a panel, or adoption of reports. Another interesting point to look at is the duration of the processes. Most incidents (44%) took more than five years to settle. Another important point to consider is the non-representation of Low-Income Food-Deficit Countries (LIFDCs) in the DSM. The LIFDC classification is based on three criteria: GNI per capita, net food export, and self-exclusion request.[12] Being self-sufficient in food can secure stricter food safety practices, which, in turn, can lead to food safety-related disputes among trading partners. The lack of LIFDCs in the DSM as complainants or respondents indicates that food insecurity presents an obstacle for food safety concerns. This situation highlights the importance of technical support and capacity development toward the participation of low-income developing countries in the DSM process. Further analysis of the DSM in terms of self-sufficiency and interaction as a complainant or respondent reveals that some of the high-income developed countries with negative net exports and low-income countries can be both complainants and respondents.

Developing countries are not homogeneous, and the under-utilization of the Dispute Settlement Mechanism highlights the need for low-income developing countries to build their capacity. The Aid for Trade initiative led by the WTO can play a significant role in capacity development. This initiative aims to mobilize resources to alleviate trade-related constraints faced by developing countries and encourages donors to support recipients' requests in the context of trade-related capacity building. Trade capacity enhancement can involve improving infrastructure, providing custom officials technical support, and offering training on trade-related entrepreneurship in collaboration with various international organizations.[13] Developing countries also need to develop their capacity in terms of legal aspects and procedures in order to participate efficiently in the DSM. In particular, these countries need financial and institutional guidance related to the costs of dispute settlement and international cooperation in establishing transparent standards in line with the guidelines set by the WTO.[14] In this context, developing countries can use the WTO's trade-related technical assistance and training (TRTA) program to build and improve their technical capacities.

Notes

1 See WTO (2023c).
2 For a detailed information on the subject see WTO, *Agriculture*, (2009).
3 Ibid.
4 See WTO, *Agriculture*, (2023d).
5 See WTO, *Doha Development Agenda*, (2023e).
6 M. Smeets, "Trade capacity building in the WTO: Main achievements since Doha and key Challenges," *Journal of World Trade*, 47(5), (2013):1047–1090.
7 Matias E. Margulis, "Negotiating from the margins: How the UN shapes the rules of the WTO," *Review of International Political Economy*, 25(3), (2018):364–391.
8 Gisele Schmid, "Technology transfer in the CDM: The role of host-country characteristics," *Climate Policy*, 12(6), (2012):722–740.
9 J. De Melo, J-M. Solleder, "Barriers to trade in environmental goods: How important they are and what should developing countries expect from their removal," World *Development*, 130, (2020):104910, 1–11.
10 WTO, *Dispute Settlement*, (2022a).
11 Cemal Atici, "Use of the dispute settlement mechanism of the WTO by developing countries in the context of food safety," *Global Trade and Customs Journal*, 13(3), (2018):107–115.
12 FAO, *Food Loss and Waste*, (2022).
13 WTO, *Building Trade Capacity*, (2022b).
14 Cemal Atici, "Use of the Dispute Settlement Mechanism," 107–115.

References

Atici, C. (2018). Use of the dispute settlement mechanism of the WTO by developing countries in the context of food safety. *Global Trade and Customs Journal*, 13(3), 107–115.

FAO (2022). Food Loss and Food Waste. https://www.fao.org/policy-support/policy-themes/food-loss-food-waste/en/ [Accessed October 4, 2022].

Margulis, M.E. (2018). Negotiating from the margins: How the UN shapes the rules of the WTO. *Review of International Political Economy*, 25(3), 364–391.

de Melo J., Solleder, J-M. (2020). Barriers to trade in environmental goods: How important they are and what should developing countries expect from their removal. *World Development*, 130, 104910, 1–11.

Schmid, G. (2012). Technology transfer in the CDM: The role of host-country characteristics. *Climate Policy*, 12(6), 722–740.

Smeets, M. (2013). Trade capacity building in the WTO: Main achievements since Doha and key challenges. *Journal of World Trade*, 47(5), 1047–1090.

WTO (2009). Agriculture. WTO Agreement Series. Geneva.

WTO (2022a). Dispute Settlement. https://www.wto.org/english/tratop_e/dispu_e/dispu_e.htm [Accessed Oct ober 27, 2022].

WTO (2022b). Building Trade Capacity https://www.wto.org/english/tratop_e/devel_e/build_tr_capa_e.htm [Accessed October 27, 2022].

WTO (2023c). https://www.wto.org [Accessed September 21, 2023].

WTO (2023d). Agriculture. https://www.wto.org/english/tratop_e/agric_e/agric_e.htm [Accessed September 5, 2023].

WTO (2023e). Doha Development Agenda. https://www.wto.org/english/thewto_e/whatis_e/tif_e/doha1_e.htm [Accessed September 18, 2023].

Part VI

Related Drivers of Sustainable Food Trade

17 Local Drivers of Sustainable Food Trade

Some effective local drivers influence the sustainable food trade, such as geographical indications, good agricultural practices (GAP), entrepreneurship, and farmer organizations. The interactions are presented in Table 17.1.

Local production activities can contribute to trade and growth if accompanied by adequate support for the main drivers of rural development. The geographical indications improve the recognition, the value of the related commodity, and the competitiveness in the value chain. The GIs can both have trade creation and trade-diverting effects. For instance, the protection of GIs creates trade when the importing and exporting countries have GI-protected products, but it has a trade-diverting effect when the importing country does not have GIs.[1] In addition, the GIs positively affect export prices because consumers perceive the GI products as higher quality.[2] The GIs, in sum, contribute to rural development through high producer income and global recognition and competitiveness.

GAP play an important role in sustainable development using sustainable methods in production. The GAP can also serve as an instrument to enhance competitiveness. The local initiatives related to the GAP in cash crops can increase the export earnings of net food-exporting developing countries. However, if the GAP is not reflected in the prices due to marketing problems, farmer incomes may not be as high as expected due to decreased production. For instance, converting from conventional agriculture to GAP may decrease yields and gross profits for some regions.[3] In addition, the lack of access to farm credits and the high cost of farm inputs may be the major constraints to compliance with global standards for developing countries.[4] Therefore, the link between the GAP and trade can be strengthened through extension, farming organizations, certification, and appropriate marketing mix in order to attain the expected income rise for the producers.

Entrepreneurship in agriculture has promising opportunities for rural development. Entrepreneurship can improve the rural economy through new products or marketing strategies, dealing with climate change, and

DOI: 10.4324/9781032708577-7

Table 17.1 Local Drivers of Sustainable Food Trade

Dynamic	Impact	Constraints to Trade, Tradeoffs
Geographical Indication	Recognition, Improved Marketing, Value chain, Trade creation/diversion, Regional development	Inequal bilateral trade earnings in case of lack of GIs in importing countries
Good Agricultural Practices	Ecology, Environmental Protection, Certification, Improved marketing, Trade	Lack of access to financing, inefficiencies in extension, farmer organizations, and marketing
Entrepreneurship	Income level, Multifunctionality	Lack of access to financing, need for public-private partnership
Farmer Organizations	Value chain, income, facilitation of new technologies through cooperative extension, support of smallholders, stakeholder participation	Management costs, low demand for certified products, lack of appropriate incentives, public-private partnership

environmentally friendly production systems. For instance, multifunctional farming-related energy production can provide more sustainable livelihoods for farmers by increasing social, economic, and environmental sustainability.[5]

Farmer organizations can increase production efficiency by providing inputs at lower costs, better accessing financial resources, and training their members for sustainable production in partnership with public or private organizations. In international trade, farmer organizations can serve as major stakeholders in sustainability policies such as the certification of exported commodities. However, appropriate financial incentives are important[6] for these types of policies' success, especially in food-exporting developing countries. The adoption of innovations can provide a higher level of income and sustainable development.[7]

18   Sustainable Consumption and Trade

Sustainable consumption, as well as production, is a major driver for sustainable development. Various factors affect sustainable consumption, such as environmental concerns, level of awareness, carbon labeling, and government policies. For instance, an environmental concern may strongly influence behavioral intention and, in turn, sustainable consumption behavior.[8] Since the consumption stage in some agricultural products has a high share in the supply chain and greenhouse gas emissions (GHGs), important reductions may be achieved in an individual's diet when purchasing and consuming food products. For this purpose, the correct environmental guidelines through awareness campaigns are essential.[9] Environmental indications on the food market, such as carbon labeling, can increase awareness of the food products consumed towards climate-certified products.[10]

Another important point to consider is the level of consumption. Consumption should be adequate such that it meets the need for a balanced diet, and overconsumption should be avoided. Food loss and food waste are the main impediments to sustainable development. It not only leads to excessive budgetary expenses but also leads to unbalanced consumption patterns in a society. Estimates suggest that approximately 14% of the world's food is lost annually between harvest and retail marketing,[11] and around 17% of the world's total food is wasted during retail and consumption. In addition, around 10% of GHGs are associated with food waste.[12] Can trade play a role in alleviating food waste? A study examining the trade-food loss/waste interaction[13] found that reductions in food losses and wastes in developed regions decrease the number of undernourished people in developing regions, leading to decreases in the harvested area, water utilization, and GHGs associated with food production. This situation occurs because of the decline in world prices and the increase in the purchasing power of consumers in developing countries.

Notes

1 Zakaria Sorgho, Bruno Larue, "Geographical indication regulation and intra-trade in the European Union," *Agricultural Economics*, 45, (2014):1–12.
2 Valentina Raimondi, et al., "Trade effects of geographical indication policy: The EU case," *Journal of Agricultural Economics*, 71(2), (2020):330–356.
3 Osman Kilic, et al., "Comparison of conventional and good agricultural practices farms: A socio-economic and technical perspective," *Journal of Cleaner Production*, 258(120666), (2020):1–9.
4 Baah P. Annor, et al., "Compliance with GLOBALGAP standards among smallholder pineapple farmers in Akuapem-South, Ghana," *Journal of Agribusiness in Developing and Emerging Economies*, 6(1), (2016):21–38.
5 Suvi Huttunen, "Wood energy production, sustainable farming livelihood and multifunctionality in Finland," *Journal of Rural Studies*, 28(4), (2012):549–558.
6 Anna Snider, et al., "Small farmer cooperatives and voluntary coffee certifications: Rewarding progressive farmers of engendering widespread change in Costa Rica?" *Food Policy*, 69, (2017):231–242.
7 Doris Lapple, Fiona Thorne, "The role of innovation in farm economic sustainability: Generalised propensity score evidence from Irish dairy farms," *Journal of Agricultural Economics*, 70(1), (2019):178–197.
8 Ulla A. Saari, et al., "Sustainable consumption behavior of Europeans: The influence of environmental knowledge and risk perception on environmental concern and behavioral intention," *Ecological Economics*, 189, (2021):1–14.
9 Ian Vazques-Rowe, et al., "The role of consumer purchase and post-purchase decision-making in sustainable seafood consumption. A Spanish case study using carbon foot printing," *Food Policy*, 41, (2013):94–102.
10 Katarina Elofsson, et al., "The impact of climate information on milk demand: Evidence from a field experiment," *Food Policy*, 58, (2016):14–23.

11 FAO, *Food Loss and Waste*, (2022).
12 UNEP, *Food Waste Index Report*, (2021).
13 Yosuke Munesue, et al., "The effects of reducing food losses and food waste on global food insecurity, natural resources, and greenhouse gas emissions," *Environmental Economics and Policy Studies*, 17, (2015):43–77.

References

Annor, B.P., Mensah-Bonsu, A., Jatoe, J.B.D. (2016). Compliance with GLOBALGAP standards among smallholder pineapple farmers in Akuapem-South, Ghana. *Journal of Agribusiness in Developing and Emerging Economies*, 6(1), 21–38.

Elofsson, K., Bengtsson, N., Matsdotter, E., Arntyr, J. (2016). The impact of climate information on milk demand: Evidence from a field experiment. *Food Policy*, 58, 14–23.

FAO (2022). Food Loss and Waste. https://www.fao.org/nutrition/capacity-development/food-loss-and-waste/en/ [Accessed November 11, 2022].

Huttunen, S. (2012). Wood energy production, sustainable farming livelihood and multifunctionality in Finland. *Journal of Rural Studies*, 28(4), 549–558.

Kilic, O., Boz, I., Eryilmaz, G.A. (2020). Comparison of conventional and good agricultural practices farms: A socio-economic and technical perspective. *Journal of Cleaner Production*, 258(120666), 1–9.

Lapple, D., Thorne, F. (2019). The role of innovation in farm economic sustainability: Generalised propensity score evidence from Irish dairy farms. *Journal of Agricultural Economics*, 70(1), 178–197.

Munesue, Y., Masui, T., Fushima, T. (2015). The effects of reducing food losses and food waste on global food insecurity, natural resources, and greenhouse gas emissions. *Environmental Economics and Policy Studies*, 17, 43–77.

Raimondi, V., Falco, C., Curzi, D., Olper, A. (2020). Trade effects of geographical indication policy: The EU case. *Journal of Agricultural Economics*, 71(2), 330–356.

Saari, U.A., Damberg, S., Frombling, L., Ringle, C.M. (2021). Sustainable consumption behavior of Europeans: The influence of environmental knowledge and risk perception on environmental concern and behavioral intention. *Ecological Economics*, 189, 1–14.

Snider, A., Gutierrez, I., Sibelet, N., Faure, G. (2017). Small farmer cooperatives and voluntary coffee certifications: Rewarding progressive farmers of engendering widespread change in Costa Rica? *Food Policy*, 69, 231–242.

Sorgho, Z., Larue, B. (2014). Geographical indication regulation and intra-trade in the European Union. *Agricultural Economics*, 45, 1–12.

UNEP (2021). Food Waste Index Report. https://www.unep.org/resources/report/unep-food-waste-index-report-2021 [Accessed October 26, 2022].

Vazquez-Rowe, I., Villanueva-Rey, P., Moreira, M.T., Feijoo, G. (2013). The role of consumer purchase and post-purchase decision-making in sustainable seafood consumption. A Spanish case study using carbon foot printing. *Food Policy*, 41, 94–102.

Part VII

Impact Evaluation and Food Trade

19 Sustainable Development and Impact Evaluation

Impact evaluation considers the possible costs and benefits of various policies and projects and involves quantitative and qualitative approaches. There are mainly two quantitative approaches in impact evaluation: ex-post versus ex-ante impact evaluations. The ex-ante impact evaluations aim to predict the possible impact of related policies and involve simulations. On the other hand, the ex-post impact evaluations aim to measure the actual impacts after the policy implementation and involve treatment effects. The ex-post impact evaluation employs various methods such as randomized evaluations, matching, double-differencing, instrumental variables, regression discontinuity, distributional impacts, and structural modeling.[1]

19.1 Sustainability Impact Assessment of Trade Agreements

The sustainability impact assessment (SIA) of trade agreements is conducted to measure the potential economic, environmental, and social impacts of these agreements. There are currently 354 regional trade agreements (RTAs) in force;[2] therefore, it is essential to know the environmental and ecological impacts of these trade agreements to better understand and evaluate the impacts and design sustainable policies thereafter. Trade SIAs usually employ a mix of quantitative, qualitative, and hybrid methods in evaluating a comprehensive set of outcomes.[3] The comparison of these methods is presented in Table 19.1.

So far, we have concentrated on the economic and environmental implications of trade policies at an aggregate level. However, it should be noted that there are certain environmental factors that affect the land, water, and air quality after the implementation of trade policies on a product basis. For instance, a study examining the retaliatory agricultural tariffs on soybeans found that such policies can cause stresses imposed by different crop production portfolios. These policies increase nitrogen and phosphorus pollution in exporting countries due to the shift from soybeans and nitrogen-fixing plants

DOI: 10.4324/9781032708577-8

Table 19.1 Sustainability Impact Assessment of Trade Agreements Tools

Method	Merits	Limitations	Comments
Quantitative			
Computable General Equilibrium (CGE)	Comprehensive, Objective, Robust Information, Simulation Capacity	Data Aggregation, Aggregation of Sustainability Criteria, Limitations on Non-Tariff Measures, Limitations on Product Base Modeling	Complementing the CGE models with PE and Case Studies
Partial Equilibrium (PE)	Objective, Policy Relevant, Easier to implement	Non-informative on general outcomes	Using certain outputs such as price changes of CGE models in PE simulations
Econometrics	Objective, can be used to evaluate the specific outcomes of trade agreements, such as FDI and technology diffusion, useful for ex-post evaluation	Non-informative on general outcomes. The main limitation is the difficulty of obtaining causal estimates of the parameters of interest and isolating the impact of trade policy from other factors that affect trade and sustainability outcomes simultaneously	Can complement other quantitative approaches
Casual Chain Analysis (CCA)	Linking the outcomes of quantitative models to sustainability outcomes	Excessive reliance on qualitative inference-based assessments	A more systematic and comprehensive approach, supported by quantitative indicators and methodologies can improve the robustness of this method
Field Research	Depth in Analysis, Survey	Selection Bias, Localized	Can be used to find sector-specific solutions
Case Studies	Local experts, Understanding Local Concerns, Detailed data	Non-informative on general outcomes	Can be used to find sector-specific solutions
Qualitative			
Regulatory-Legal Analysis Stakeholder Consultation	Mapping the current issues Local inputs for the issue	Theory-Reality Issues Ensuring the representativeness and comprehensiveness of stakeholder engagement	

Source: Compiled from Moise and Rubinova, 2021

Table 19.2 Possible Environmental Impacts of Crop-Specific Liberalized Trade Policies

	Land	*Water*	*Air*
Importing Country	-Nitrogen Level of Soil [N-fixing plants] -Less Chemical Use	-Water Conservation	-Less Air Pollution
Exporting Country	-Nitrogen Level of Soil [N-fixing plants] -Excessive Chemical Use	-Excessive Water Use	-Air Pollution

to more pollution-causing crops. In addition, if import demand shifts from one country to another due to political reasons, it may add additional pressure on deforestation.[4] When importing country converts from nitrogen (N)-fixing crops such as soybeans to N-demanding crops such as wheat, corn, and rice, nitrogen pollution may increase;[5] therefore, the choice of crop cultivation should be examined carefully.

The specific environmental impacts of food trade policies are presented in Table 19.2. If an importing country liberalizes its trade, it may protect the environment using less chemicals, less irrigation, and air polluting inputs. Still, environmental degradation may occur due to the loss of nitrogen-efficient crops. On the other hand, when an exporting country exports specific crops due to higher trade, the nitrogen-efficient crops improve the land quality; however, the use of polluting inputs such as chemicals and excessive use of irrigation harms the environment due to overproduction. Countries producing and trading food using aquifers intensely may cause the depletion of these water resources rapidly.[6] The total water footprints of agricultural products vary by product. For instance, these values are 1826 m^3 for wheat, 14431 m^3 for olive oil, 15415 m^3 for bovine meat, and 15897 m^3 for coffee.[7] In some countries, the tradeoff between food self-sufficiency, such as producing staple food, and economic efficiency, such as employment, can put pressure on natural resources, demanding the use of higher inputs and resources.[8] Air pollution in agriculture is mainly caused by the use of fertilizers and livestock production in the form of ammonia and methane emissions and by the use of fossil energy inputs in the form of carbon emissions. Based on the current level of climate change, an efficient use of natural resources and developing appropriate adaptation and mitigation strategies in a holistic manner should be a priority in domestic and international agendas.

Notes

1 For a detailed information on the impact evaluation methodologies see Khandker et al. (2010).

2 WTO, *Regional Trade Agreements,* (2022).
3 Evdokia Moise, Stela Rubínova, "Sustainability impact assessments of free trade agreements: A critical review," *OECD Trade Policy Papers,* No. 255, (Paris: OECD Publishing, 2021).
4 Guolin Yao, et al., "The increasing global environmental consequences of a weakening US–China crop trade relationship," *Nature Food,* 2(8), (2021):578–586.
5 Jing Sun, et al., "Importing food damages domestic environment: Evidence from global soybean trade," *PNAS,* 115(21), (2018):5415–5419.
6 Carole Dalin, et al., "Groundwater depletion embedded in international food trade," *Nature,* 543(7647), (2017):700–704.
7 For a detailed information on the issue see Mekonnen and Hoekstra, 2010a, 2010b.
8 Rashid M. Hassan, et al., "The trade-off between economic efficiency and food self-sufficiency in using Sudan's irrigated land resources," *Food Policy,* 25(1), (2000):35–54.

References

Dalin, C., Wada, Y., Kastner, T., Puma, M.J., (2017). Groundwater depletion embedded in international food trade. *Nature,* 543(7647), 700–704.

Hassan, R.M., Faki, H., Byerlee, D. (2000). The trade-off between economic efficiency and food self-sufficiency in using Sudan's irrigated land resources. *Food Policy,* 25(1), 35–54.

Khandker, S.R., Koolwal, G.B., Samad, H.A. (2010). *Handbook on Impact Evaluation Quantitative Methods and Practices.* Washington, DC: The World Bank.

Mekonnen, M.M., Hoekstra, A.Y. (2010a). The Green, Blue and Grey Water Footprint of Crops and Derived Crop Products. Value of Water Research Report Series, No:48. DA Delft. UNESCO-IHE Institute for Water Education.

Mekonnen, M.M., Hoekstra, A.Y. (2010b). The Green, Blue and Grey Water Footprint of Farm Animals and Animal Products. Value of Water Research Report Series, No:47. DA Delft. UNESCO-IHE Institute for Water Education.

Moise, E., Rubínova, S. (2021), Sustainability impact assessments of free trade agreements: A critical review, *OECD Trade Policy Papers,* No. 255. Paris: OECD Publishing.

Sun, J., Mooney, H. Wu, W., Tang, H., Tong, Y., Xu, Z., Huang, B., Cheng, Y., Yang, X., Wei, D., Zhang, F., Liu, J. (2018). Importing food damages domestic environment: Evidence from global soybean trade. *PNAS,* 115(21), 5415–5419.

WTO (2022). Regional trade agreements. https://www.wto.org/english/tratop_e/region_e/region_e.htm [Accessed November 9, 2022].

Yao, G., Zhang, X., Davidson, E.A., Taheripour, F. (2021). The increasing global environmental consequences of a weakening US–China crop trade relationship. *Nature Food,* 2(8), 578–586.

Part VIII

Sustainable Development Goals, Indicators, and Food Trade

20   Sustainable Development Goals and Trade

Trade can play a significant role in delivering key sustainable development goals (SDGs).[1] The interaction with selected SDGs can be described as follows:

SDG1, No Poverty: Trade liberalization can contribute to economic growth through productivity, competition, and low prices for consumers. As described before, such trade liberalization policies' benefits depend on efficient policy designs that consider environmental and equity concerns.

SDG2, Zero Hunger: Eliminating or decreasing subsidies implemented in agricultural trade can reduce market distortions and contribute to food security. For certain, implementing these policies requires a multilateral approach and the concerns of developing countries.

SDG3, *Good Health and Well-being*: The WTO's Trade-Related Intellectual Property Rights (TRIPS) Agreement can enable developing countries to access secure and legal health products. However, a careful policy design is necessary in order to avoid new trade protectionist mechanisms.

SDG5, Gender Equality: Trade can create job opportunities for women. Women's participation in the labor force can contribute to rural development. Concerns related to the formalization of trade, especially in low-income developing countries, should be addressed in collaboration with national and international stakeholders. The inclusiveness of gender-related preferential trade agreements (PTAs) can promote cooperation among developing countries on gender issues.

SDG8, Decent Work and Economic Growth: Obviously, trade can contribute to economic growth. In that context, the Aid for Trade initiative can help developing countries improve their trade potential.

SDG9, Industry, Innovation, and Infrastructure: Trade can contribute to economic development through competition and the transfer of technology, knowledge, and innovation.

SDG10, Reduced Inequalities: There are certain capacity constraints among the countries. As mentioned before, the distributional effect of trade

DOI: 10.4324/9781032708577-9

varies depending on the structure of an economy. Special and differential treatment for developing countries can allow the use of flexibilities by developing and least-developed countries to consider their capacity constraints.

SDG13, Climate Action: Agriculture plays a major role in the economies of low-income and middle-income developing countries, and the inclusion of that sector in climate agreements, such as flexibility mechanisms, might be on the agenda. High transaction costs and immature financial markets are the main obstacles to be addressed. The issues arising from the structural problems of developing countries should be tackled in tandem with the flexibility mechanisms of climate agreements through technical assistance and capacity building.

SDG14, Life Below Water: The Decision on Fisheries Subsidies taken by WTO members in 2017 aims to prohibit subsidies that contribute to overcapacity and overfishing and eliminate subsidies that contribute to illegal, unreported, and unregulated fishing, considering special and differential treatment for developing and least-developed countries.

SDG15, Life on Land: Protecting, restoring, and sustainable use of ecosystems, sustainable management of natural resources, and halting biodiversity loss require both domestic and international policy designs, such as setting and monitoring regulations related to production, consumption, and trade of natural resources.

SDG17, Partnerships for the Goals: Implementing a successful sustainable development policy requires international partnership. In that context, the concerns of developing countries and international cooperation in specific areas, such as the Flexibility Mechanisms of climate agreements, are necessary.

21   Sustainable Development Indicators and Trade

There are certain frameworks to measure and compare sustainable development performances and sustainable development indicators (SDIs) that measure the performances of countries and sectors in achieving sustainable development over the period. The main framework for SDIs is The UN Statistical Commission's System of Environmental-Economic Accounting (SEEA), and the main indicators are the Sustainable Development Solutions Network's Sustainable Development Gola Index (SDG Index), Sustainable Development Index (SDI), and Environmental Performance Index (EPI).

The SEEA constructs an integrated and comprehensive statistical framework for organizing data about habitats and landscapes, measuring the ecosystem services, tracking changes in ecosystem assets, and linking this information to economic and other human activity.[2] The accounts measured in the SEEA are ecosystem extent, ecosystem condition, ecosystem services, and monetary ecosystem assets. The ecosystem extent account records the total area of the ecosystem by nation, province, river basin, and protected areas by ecosystem type over the period. The ecosystem condition records the condition of ecosystem assets based on selected characteristics. The ecosystem services account records the supply of ecosystem services by ecosystem assets and their use by economic units. The monetary ecosystem asset account records stock information and changes such as degradation and enhancement. The SEEA covers certain trade issues, such as trade in biomass products and trade of wild species.

The SDG Index is constructed by the UN Sustainable Development Solutions Network.[3] It mainly constructs an index for countries based on the performances of the 2030 Agenda for Sustainable Development[4] and SDGs. The SDG Index also incorporates trade-related issues such as the export of plastic waste per capita, the logistic performance index, and CO_2 emissions embodied in fossil fuel exports (kg/capita).

The SDI measures the ecological efficiency of the countries incorporating the Human Development Index (HDI).[5] It covers various factors such as life expectancy, expected years of schooling, income per capita, CO2 emissions per capita, and material footprint per capita. The EPI utilizes 40 indicators across 11 issue categories.[6] The categories include climate change mitigation, air quality, sanitation and drinking water, heavy metals, waste management, biodiversity and habitat, ecosystem services, fisheries, acid rain, agriculture, and water resources.

Based on the evaluation of these indices, it can be asserted that only the UN SDG Index covers some aspects of trade activities. Given the fact that trade impacts the environment through transportation-led emission levels and scale effect, future calculations should consider the trade-environment interaction at the sectoral level in order to design sector-specific policies.

Notes

1 For a detailed discussion on the issue see WTO (2022).
2 See UN, *Ecosystem Accounting*, (2022).
3 See UNSDSN, *Sustainable Development Solutions Network*, (2022).
4 See UN SDGS, *Sustainable Development*, (2022).
5 See Jason Hickel, "The sustainable development index: Measuring the ecological efficiency of human development in the anthropocene," *Ecological Economics*, 167, (2020):1–10.
6 See Martin J. Wolf, et al., *Environmental Performance Index* (New Haven, CT: Yale Center for Environmental Law & Policy, 2022).

References

Hickel, J. (2020). The sustainable development index: Measuring the ecological efficiency of human development in the anthropocene. *Ecological Economics*, 167, 1–10.
UN (2022). Ecosystem Accounting. https://seea.un.org/ecosystem-accounting [Accessed December 19, 2022].

UN SDGS (2022). Sustainable Development. https://sdgs.un.org/ [Accessed December 19, 2022].

UNSDSN (2022). Sustainable Development Solutions Network. https://www.unsdsn.org/ [Accessed December 19, 2022].

Wolf, M.J., Emerson, J.W., Esty, D.C., de Sherbinin, A., Wendling, Z.A., et al. (2022). *2022 Environmental Performance Index*. New Haven, CT: Yale Center for Environmental Law & Policy. https://epi.yale.edu/ [Accessed November 25, 2022].

WTO (2022). The WTO and Sustainable Development Goals. https://www.wto.org/english/thewto_e/coher_e/sdgs_e/sdgs_e.htm [Accessed January 5, 2023].

Part IX

Macroeconomics and Sustainable Development

22   Macroeconomics of the Sustainable Policies

Trade and macroeconomic indicators, such as economic growth and economic policies, are interrelated. In one of the trade-growth interaction studies[1], it was found that trade has a quantitatively large and positive impact on growth. Trade raises income through the accumulation of physical and human capital and the output given the capital levels. In terms of food trade, it was found that agricultural trade played a crucial role in the structural transformation of various countries.[2] Therefore, an increase in the food trade is expected to raise income levels, especially for developing countries whose exports mainly depend on agriculture-related sectors.

Unfortunately, macroeconomics has not utilized environmental concerns in policy analysis for a long time, similar to the other conventional branches of economics. However, recent studies have attempted to utilize the environmental concern in the macro policy analysis. Heyes[3] extended the conventional (IS-LM) framework to include the environmental equilibrium (EE). The framework is basically used to examine the interaction between goods and money markets and the level of aggregate income. The EE curve assumes that the rate at which the economy uses environmental services is equal to the environment's ability to compensate. For instance, in the case of emissions, the aggregate rate of emissions must equal the rate at which the environment can absorb the emission level. That way, the impacts of macro policies are in line with sustainable development. This situation is depicted in Figure 22.1.

In the setting, Y represents the real income and R represents the long-term real interest rate. A fiscal expansion shifts the IS curve to the right but does not lead to EE. In order to achieve the EE, fiscal expansion must be accompanied by a monetary contraction. In that situation, the LM curve shifts to the left, leading to a lower level of Y.

Lawn[4] extended the IS-LM-EE model to include technology such that the EE curve is a function of resource-saving and pollution-reducing technological progress. In that situation, any expansionary fiscal policy leads to a rightward shift of the IS curve followed by the required contractionary monetary

DOI: 10.4324/9781032708577-10

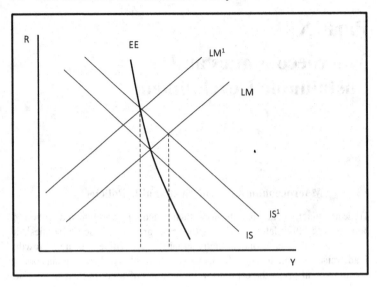

Figure 22.1 The Fiscal Expansion and Environmental Equilibrium
Source: Reproduced with the permission of Heyes, 2000.

policy depicted by the leftward shift of the LM curve. That way, the new environmental-macroeconomic equilibrium occurs. However, when technological progress is considered, the equilibrium changes depending on the level of the progress. If there is no technological progress, the EE curve will maintain its original position, while higher resource costs and higher good prices will reduce the supply of real money balance. However, the EE curve shifts rightward if there is resource-saving technological progress. The rise of input prices is less than the case of no technological progress, and the LM curve displays a smaller shift leftward. Therefore, the new environmental-macroeconomic equilibrium occurs with a slight loss of the Y. This situation is presented in Figure 22.2.

In agriculture, trade costs in input and output markets have an essential role in determining technology adoption such that in the presence of high trade costs, subsidy programs may reduce producer welfare despite the increased production. Therefore, technology adoption strategies, especially in developing countries, can be linked to trade cost reduction initiatives.[5] Since macro policies impact all economic sectors, including agriculture, any expansionary policy should consider the environmental impacts in policy design. The implementation of this framework for developing countries has several implications. Given the fact that growth is essential to improve welfare and decrease unemployment, such contractionary policies may not be preferable

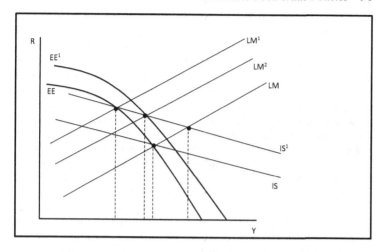

Figure 22.2 The Fiscal Expansion and Environmental Equilibrium with Technological
    Progress

Source: Reproduced with the permission of Lawn, 2003.

from the political economy point of view. On the other hand, the agricultural sector has an important weight in the economies of developing countries, and this sector needs to be supported in order to prevent possible social and economic problems. As might be expected, growth policies in specific sectors need to consider environmental concerns and to achieve sustainable development goals. Consequently, the optimal strategy design may include setting priority areas in an economy accompanied by incentives for technological progress and implementing macro environmental policies based on these priorities. The policies can include incentives for the use of specific technologies and standards, emission abatement subsidies for cleaner energy, and institutional design towards control and monitoring of the policies implemented. That way, the efficient use of limited resources can be achieved.

23   Macroeconomics and Sustainable Food
       Trade Policies

The main macroeconomic variables that impact trade flow and sustainable food trade are income levels of reporting and partner countries, exchange rates, volatility, oil and energy prices, trade costs (transportation, trade policies such as tariffs, information cost, etc.), and non-tariff measures (NTMs). Since GDP per capita represents a good proxy for the level of development and purchasing power, it is widely utilized in trade flow analysis, and the per capita incomes of reporting and partner countries positively impact the export flow. Price volatilities in food products are especially harmful to developing countries because of food inflation, deteriorating terms of trade, increased input costs, and aggravating poverty.[6] Exchange rates play a significant role in bilateral trade flow. Changes in exchange rates impact export and input prices, affecting export competitiveness. An appreciation of the domestic exchange rates leads to higher prices for export markets and may decrease exports. Exchange rate volatility, on the other hand, is another issue in international trade. An increase in exchange rate volatility is usually associated with a reduced volume of trade flow caused by the risk-averse structure of the trading firms, and it affects trade flow through uncertainty and adjustment costs. An increase in oil and energy prices has a twofold impact on trade flow. Any observed increase in world oil prices lead to higher cost in agricultural production and may result in less production, leading to less trade flow and higher commodity prices in the medium run. On the other hand, high oil prices lead to higher transportation costs and may deter bilateral trade flow, especially for distant partners. Tariff rates are barriers to trade and, therefore, negatively affect the trade flow. NTMs are gaining as trade barriers recently as conventional trade barriers such as tariffs are liberalized in the multilateral trading system.

The impacts of both price and exchange rate volatilities have different impacts on the agricultural sector compared to the other sectors. Agricultural price volatility transmissions are more common in developing countries with higher trade dependence.[7] Although exchange rate volatility is usually considered a trade-impeding factor, exporting firms can benefit from an increase in exchange rate volatility by optimally adjusting their export volumes to the level of exchange rates.[8] The response of the agricultural sector, on the other hand, is usually negative compared to the other sectors. Agricultural exports may be negatively affected by a high frequency of exchange rate fluctuations compared to the other sectors in an economy, especially in the short run.[9] Real exchange rate uncertainty has a significant negative effect on agricultural trade flow, and this effect is higher in the agricultural sector.[10] In addition, countries with higher rates of exchange rate volatility have higher pass-through elasticities.[11]

The use of financial hedging instruments such as forward exchange rate contracts, currency swaps, and dynamic hedging strategies, such as option pricing, can reduce exporting firms' vulnerability caused by volatile currency movements. Whether the agricultural sector in developing countries benefits from these financial instruments depends on many macroeconomic factors. It should be underlined that establishing such a financial system is not an easy task, especially in least developed countries (LDCs), and it requires a certain level of investment in human capital and financial infrastructure. Developing countries, including the LDCs, can utilize the futures markets as a hedging instrument[12] to protect their agricultural export earnings, provided that the legal and regulatory system is well-defined and supported by a well-functioning financial system.

Many studies confirmed the negative impact of conventional protection levels on agricultural trade flow[13] and implied improved welfare impacts for further agricultural trade reforms in developing countries.[14] Globalized value chains may have an impact on unconventional trade protection policies. Global value chain integration, measured as value added in final goods, affects food trade policy, such as reducing trade barriers through lobbying and government incentives.[15] The reduction in conventional and trade barriers and adequate use of the NTMs can assure food safety and security for consumers, especially in low-income countries. However, trade liberalization efforts should be in tandem with domestic agricultural policies, assuring adequate income levels for producers, protecting environmental quality, and achieving sustainable development goals in the long run. In that sense, multilateral cooperation and capacity development are necessary for designing optimal policies.

Macroeconomic policies can be designed to achieve sustainable development in developing countries. Green macroeconomic policies, such as issuing green bonds, and green monetary policies, such as financing for related projects, can be used to fund projects that improve environmental quality and the welfare of producers in agricultural sectors. Studies on macro environmental policies and green finance instruments (issuance of green bonds) show that these policies affect green resource performance positively. At the same time, changes in oil prices and regional uncertainties have a harmful impact on investments in renewable energy.[16] Sustainable development requires micro and macro perspectives in designing sustainable policies, especially in food and agriculture. Macro policies are especially important in allocating budgetary expenditures and specifying priorities. These policies should be implemented in tandem with the micro-level policies and should be inclusive, covering all related stakeholders involved in the process. Eventually, international responsibility and collaboration are required to achieve the design, implementation, and monitoring of efficient sustainable development policies.

Notes

1 Jeffrey A. Frankel, David H. Romer, "Does trade cause growth?" *The American Economic Review*, 89(3), (1999):379–399.
2 Marc Teignier, "The role of trade in structural transformation," *Journal of Development Economics*, 130, (2018):45–65.
3 Anthony Heyes, "A proposal for the greening of textbook macro: IS-LM-EE," *Ecological Economics*, 32, (2020):1–7.
4 Philip A. Lawn, "On Heyes' IS-LM-EE proposal to establish an environmental macroeconomics," *Environment and Development Economies*, 8, (2003):31–56.
5 Obie Porteous, "Trade and agricultural technology adoption: Evidence from Africa," *Journal of Development Economics*, 144(2020):102440.
6 Philip Abbott, de Battisti A.B. "Recent global food price shocks: Causes, consequences and lessons for African governments and donors," *Journal of African Economies*, 20(1), (2011):12–62.

7 F. Ceballos, et al., "Grain price and volatility transmission from international to domestic markets in developing countries," *World Development*, 94, (2017):305–320.

8 Gunter Franke, "Exchange rate volatility and international trading strategy," *Journal of International Money and Finance*, 10(2), (1991):292–307.

9 Kai-Li Wang, Christopher B. Barrett, "Estimating the effects of exchange rate volatility on export volumes," *Journal of Agricultural and Resource Economics*, 32(2), (2007):225–255.

10 Guedae Cho, et al., "Exchange rate uncertainty and agricultural trade," *American Journal of Agricultural Economics*, 84(4), (2002):931–942.

11 Jose M. Campa, Linda S. Goldberg, "Exchange rate pass-through into import prices," *The Review of Economics and Statistics*, 87(4), (2005):679–690.

12 C. Wyn Morgan, et al., "Agricultural futures markets in LDCs: A policy response to price volatility?" *Journal of International Development*, 11(6), (1999):893–910.

13 Cemal Atici, et al.," Does Turkey's Integration into the European Union boost its agricultural exports?" *Agribusiness*, 27(3), (2011):280–291.

14 Kym Anderson, Will Martin, "Agricultural trade reform and the Doha Development Agenda," *World Economy*, 28(9), (2005):101–1327.

15 Valentina Raimondi, et al., "Impact of global value chains on tariffs and non-tariff measures in agriculture and food," *Food Policy*, 118(102469), (2023):1–15.

16 Xiaojing Xu, Runguo Xu, "Role of green financing and stability in the development of green resources in China," *Resources Policy*, 85(103954), (2023):1–8.

References

Abbott, P., de Battisti, A.B. (2011). Recent global food price shocks: Causes, consequences and lessons for African governments and donors. *Journal of African Economies*, 20(1), 12–62.

Anderson, K., Martin, W. (2005). Agricultural trade reform and the Doha Development Agenda. *World Economy*, 28(9), 101–1327.

Atici, C. (2011). Does Turkey's integration into the European Union boost its agricultural exports? *Agribusiness*, 27(3), 280–291.

Campa, J.M., Goldberg, S. (2005). Exchange rate pass-through into import prices. *The Review of Economics and Statistics*, 87(4), 679–690.

Ceballos, F., Hernandez, M.A., Minot, N., Robles, M. (2017). Grain price and volatility transmission from international to domestic markets in developing countries. *World Development*, 94, 305–320.

Cho, G., Sheldon, I.M., McCorriston, S. (2002). Exchange rate uncertainty and agricultural trade. *American Journal of Agricultural Economics*, 84(4), 931–942.

Franke, G. (1991). Exchange rate volatility and international trading strategy. *Journal of International Money and Finance*, 10(2), 292–307.

Frankel, J.A., Romer, D.H. (1999). Does trade cause growth? *The American Economic Review*, 89(3), 379–399.

Heyes, A. (2000). A proposal for the greening of textbook macro: IS-LM-EE. *Ecological Economics*, 32, 1–7.

Lawn, P. (2003). On Heyes' IS-LM-EE proposal to establish an environmental macroeconomics. *Environment and Development Economies*, 8, 31–56.

Morgan, C.W., Rayner, A.J., Vaillant, C. (1999). Agricultural futures markets in LDCs: A policy response to price volatility? *Journal of International Development*, 11(6), 893–910.

Porteous, O. (2020). Trade and agricultural technology adoption: Evidence from Africa. *Journal of Development Economics*, 144(2020), 102440.

Raimondi, V., Piriu, A., Swinnen, J., Olper, A. (2023). Impact of global value chains on tariffs and non-tariff measures in agriculture and food. *Food Policy*, 118(102469), 1–15.

Romer, D. (1996). *Advanced Macroeconomics*. New York: McGraw-Hill.

Teignier, M. (2018). The role of trade in structural transformation. *Journal of Development Economics*, 130, 45–65.

Wang, K-L., Barrett, C.B. (2007). Estimating the effects of exchange rate volatility on export volumes. *Journal of Agricultural and Resource Economics*, 32(2), 225–255.

Xu, X., Xu, R. (2023). Role of green financing and stability in the development of green resources in China. *Resources Policy*, 85(103954), 1–8.

Index

Note: **Bold** page numbers refer to tables and *italic* page numbers refer to figures.

Printed in the United States
by Baker & Taylor Publisher Services